LIVERPOOL CHARACTERS AND ECCENTRICS

RICHARD WHITTINGTON-EGAN

THE GALLERY PRESS
LEIGHTON BANASTRE, PARKGATE, SOUTH WIRRAL

ISBN   0   900389   22   2
Published by Gallery Press 1985   Reprinted 1989
© Richard Whittington-Egan
Printed by Scotprint (North West) Limited.

Back in the days when the Beatles would still pop into Ye Cracke in Rice Street to take a friendly ale with me, I was paying a young man's court to the fickle jade of the Mersey. I wrote two love chronicles of our on-off affair—*Liverpool Colonnade* and *Liverpool Roundabout*. Oh, I was a knight-errant then, pricking in fancy my milk-white palfrey through the stone forest and down the avenues of my imagination. And such imaginings! I saw the Liver birds take wing against a low lying hunter's moon . . . the chimney-masted tangle of sky-riding roof-tops looking at dusk like the decks of ships at swaying anchor . . . I heard the golden and porcelained names on windows singing the old crafts' songs and lullabies of trade . . . I lurked around the Western bazaar counters in the lit grottoes of the shops . . . I rode the overhead railway and the Noah's Ark tramcars . . . watched the glittering city slip over the horizon's edge into the purple pomp of night—and out again into the watered-milk light of another dawn. Both I and the Liverpool of which I wrote have grown up, grown different. We have played weather-vanes to the wind of change. And yet we are still the same at heart. The fresh wind blowing across the river and over my city's wild hilltop still whispers the old tales to those who are willing to listen . . . a light still burns in Paradise Street . . .

CONTENTS

		Page
1	The Mole of Mason Street	7
2	Solomon in All His Glory	15
3	Portrait of a Liverpool Musician	21
4	Sherlock Holmes and Liverpool	24
5	The Nine Foot 'Childe'	31
6	Queen of the Wash Houses	35
7	The Armless Midget who Painted Kings	40
8	The Story of Skittles	44
9	The Pugnacious Vicar of St. George's	48
10	The Strange Claims of Margaret M'Avoy	51
11	Hugh Owen Thomas—Surgeon Extraordinary	54
12	Sir Robert Jones—Beloved Physician	60

1. THE MOLE OF MASON STREET

One day, back in the dawn of the Railway Age, a husky gang of Irish navvies were happily hacking a tunnel through the great sandstone mass which was impeding George Stephenson's first railway line between Edge Hill and Lime Street. Suddenly, a mighty blow from one of their picks went clean through the stone floor, and, to the horror of the workmen, strange noises began to float up from the heart of the rock. Standing silent and spellbound in the eerie flicker of their lanterns, they saw the hole widen itself, and, as they watched, wide-eyed, a head popped out and addressed them in language unmistakably associated with the infernal regions! It was all too much for the superstitious Irishmen; with yelps of terror they downed tools and fled frantically for the daylight.

An old wives' tale? An unfathomable mystery? Not quite. There is an explanation. It seems that Stephenson had a rival and that his labourers had unwittingly trespassed upon the subterranean preserves of one of the most fantastic characters in the whole of Liverpool's chequered history— Joseph Williamson, the Gargantuan mole of Mason Street.

Born into poverty, on March 10th, 1769, in the neighbouring Lancashire township of Warrington, this Joseph Williamson arrived in Liverpool round about the year 1780. Provided with but a few shillings, a tin trunk of clothes and a plenitude only of parental advice, the eleven-year-old boy came hopefully to seek his fortune in the big city. It was not long before he managed to find a job in the Wolstenholme Square factory of one Thomas Moss Tate, a tobacco merchant, where he worked hard and gradually advanced to a position of considerable responsibility. Indeed, by 1802 he had so far won his master's esteem that he was permitted to marry into the family, and, on December 12th, he was wed at St. Thomas's Church, Park Lane, to Elizabeth Tate, "daughter of the late Mr. Richard Tate, Merchant." On the occasion of his marriage we are afforded a first glimpse of that eccentricity which was later to become his outstanding characteristic, for Williamson arrived at the church clad in hunting-pink, and, at the end of the ceremony, after telling his bride to be off home to get his dinner ready, he mounted his horse and galloped merrily off to a meet of the Liverpool Hunt.

Shortly after his marriage, his employer having succumbed to a surfeit of Bacchanalian delights, Joseph Williamson succeeded to the ownership of the business, and for fifteen years he applied himself assiduously to the task of acquiring a considerable fortune. In 1818 he finally retired from the hectic service of Mammon and made vast purchases of land and house property in the vicinity of Mason Street, Edge Hill. Then the fun started, and very soon Joseph Williamson had acquired a reputation for eccentricity second to none!

The principal way in which this eccentricity manifested itself seems to have been in a peculiar desire to burrow. His house in Mason Street was built upon a foundation of solid sandstone and, commencing from his own cellar, he began to excavate a series of subterranean passages and huge underground halls, which, in the fulness of time, came to form a positive maze of tortuous catacombs without parallel throughout the length and breadth of the land. At various depths between ten and fifty feet below the surface of the ground, and stretching for a total of several miles, a labyrinth of these passages wound and twisted a serpentine course through the very heart of the solid rock. There seemed neither rhyme nor reason in the construction of these tunnels; they conformed to no apparent plan and the only key to their purpose, if any, and relative spatial distribution, lay locked within the secretive mind of Williamson himself.

Access to this fantastic underworld was through a heavy, wooden door situated in Williamson's cellar. Beyond this sturdy barrier to the uninvited lay the rambling realms of Wiliamson's terrain of perpetual night; a dark, dank and sepulchral sphere of silent stone, where passage succeeded passage in an unending monotony of slimed and moss-grown solitude. But here and there the featureless regularity of this saturnine architecture was suddenly relieved by the unexpected advent of vast vaults, thirty to forty feet in width and, some, fifty feet in height. And scattered about in perilous plenitude were hungry pits and yawning chasms that seemed to cry silently for the vengeful engulfing of any who would ignore their presence. Within the halls, and likewise in the passages, sound precautions had been taken against the collapse of the kingdon by the simple expedient of vaulting the roofs with brick. But, for the trespasser, the dangers were myriad. Escaping the menace of pit and chasm, the intruder, untutored in the geography of this earthen place, where everywhere was the fungus-stench, sweet and nauseating, of corruption, and nowhere light or ventilation, might well find in it a tomb, for amidst the plethora of purposive tunnels lurked a goodly number of aimless, blank-walled and circular passages which led to nothing more than an abrupt end, or were nothing more than a circuitous route back to the initial starting point. It is not improbable that Williamson made some at least of the latter type in order that he might emerge with a fatal combination of suddenness and unexpectedness upon any dodger whom he numbered among the hosts of artisans to whom his excavations gave employment. Such motive and action are quite in character. And what of the "tumps" from the burrowings of this Gargantuan mole? It is believed that the greater part of the fine red sandstone removed by his workmen was given by Williamson for use in the building of the nearby church of St. Jude. A great deal of it was also utilised in the erection of odd arches and allied structures here and there around his property. Indeed, Williamson had something of a weakness for arches and an amusing story is recounted of how on one occasion when he was talking to a certain Liverpool minister he expressed regret that he had not been educated for the church, adding that he was quite sure that he would have attained to the dignity of a bishop. "Oh!" replied the parson, "You would certainly have deserved to be an *arch-bishop*!"

Why Williamson went to the trouble and not inconsiderable expense of making these excavations, no one will ever really know. The whole thing remains one of those delightfully insoluble problems to titillate the curiosity of the psychologist and perplex, mayhap, the imagination of some zealous antiquarian of futurity. The explanation offered by Williamson himself was that it was his way of proffering disguised charity to a necessitous poor. Indeed, it is recorded how Williamson was once sitting upon a Poor Aid Committee, the members of which irritated him by continual,oblique reference to their own charity of disposition. At last Williamson could endure it no longer. "How many of you employ labourers?" he bellowed. Dead silence. Still fuming, he shepherded the entire committee to a nearby yard which he owned and there indicated some fifty men, all busily engaged in what was apparently a series of utterly pointless tasks. Some of the labourers were carting piles of stones from one place to another, others were alternately pumping water out of, and empting it back into, a well, while yet more were occupied in an aimless turning of grindstones. To the superficial observer it would seem that all this activity was quite purposeless. Their labour was no more than the digging of a hole today and the filling of it in on the morrow; but they all received a weekly wage and were thus enabled to enjoy the blessing of charity without the attendant curse of stifled self-respect. Moreover, Williamson would often regale his men with a barrel of ale or port, a fair enough compensation for the most eccentric of orders! Likewise, in the construction of his gigantic subterranean folly Williamson gave employment to hundreds of men and, because at that time unemployment was rife as a result of the Napoleonic wars, he became famed locally as a great public benefactor. Certainly, many families had every cause to bless the erratic charity of this amazing man, for were they not indebted to his tunnel-mania for the wherewithal to purchase the meagre necessities of their lives?

They christened him the "King of Edge Hill." A shabby enough king in all conscience. His only crown, a battered beaver; his robes of office an old, patched brown coat, corduroy breeches and hobnailed boots. And this was the man who stepped forward to greet George IV when, as Prince of Wales, he visited Liverpool in, 1806, and all the city fathers seemed dumbstruck with their own unworthiness; the man of whom the prince said, "He is the only gentleman I met in Liverpool."

If Joseph Williamson bewildered those who worked for him, he was also an enigma to the people who lived in the houses which he owned and it is scarcely surprising to find that his Mason Street tenants held rather diverse views about the bedraggled eccentric who was their landlord. At one moment he woud be charming and accommodating to a degree, in another mood he would be suspicious and unyielding. A tenant asked him to build her a nursery on account of an increasing family. He resisted all entreaties. Eventually, she sent him a formal application addressed to "The King of Edge Hill." The very next morning there was a tremendous crash as part of the wall of one of here rooms came tottering down and there, as the cloud of brick dust cleared, she beheld the "King" himself who stood bowing in the jagged hole as he regally informed her that in response to her petition he had decided to accord her the use of his own drawingroom, so that she might have "the finest nursery in Liverpool."

Another tenant once complained that his house was damp. Williamson was in one of his queer moods and received the complaint churlishly. A few mornings later, however, the complainant's servant was lighting the kitchen fire when she was terrified almost into fits on seeing a considerable portion of the stone floor suddenly give way and the head and shoulders of a man start up through the hole. It ultimately transpired that the intruder was a workman and that he was engaged in making a sewer to carry off the water in an attempt to subdue the damp. Williamson had heeded after all.

Odd as a landlord, Williamson was, if possible, even odder as a neighbour. To begin with his house itself presented a number of singular features. It contained many large and lofty apartments, was furnished with doors in all manner of unexpected places and was also provided with a multitude of passages which led nowhere. Windows there were in abundance, too, many of which were quite useless as they were set on inner landings and in suchlike unprofitable situations. Latterly, the window-tax became quite an item and Williamson actually built a huge rockery outside his morning-room window in order to hide its expensive expanse. He was also, as we have said, strongly addicted to the erection of stone arches and various other structures all around the outside of his house and, at incredible expense, finally succeeded in making the whole locality too grotesque for words.

10

In the course of time the neighbours came to ignore the frequent and uncanny noises which issued from the ground below their houses and the sudden appearance of a number of men wheeling a fleet of bright blue wheelbarrows into Williamson's drawing-room excited little more than the quizzical raising of sundry eyebrows.

For all the outward ferocity and boorishness of his demeanour, there was a great deal of the mischievous schoolboy in Williamson, and he was much given to the indulgence of a somewhat bizarre sense of humour. Perhaps one of his most remarkable "jokes," and certainly the most successful, was his celebrated "Beanfeast." One day a number of local worthies were surprised to receive an invitation to dinner from Williamson. His dignified contemporaries were somewhat disconcerted upon arrival by being led into a large breakfast-room wherein a common trestle-table was sparsely laid with most inferior varieties of cutlery and crockery. Seating themselves uncomfortably around the unfestive board, they received a further shock when the removal of the dish-covers revealed an unappetising repast of beans and bacon! Many of the distinguished guests thereupon rose and left the house in high dudgeon. When they had departed Williamson turned, chuckling, and said, "Now that I know who really *are* my friends, pray follow me upstairs." In an upper chamber they reaped the reward of loyalty in the form of a really sumptuous banquet.

On Friday, May 1st, 1840, Joseph Williamson died, aged 71 years, of "water on the chest." Much to everyone's surprise he left no last instructions for a fantastic funeral and was laid quietly to rest in the Tate family vault in the yard of St. Thomas's Church, Liverpool. Fittingly enough, a man unique in life has has become unique in death, for on the demolition of St. Thomas's in 1905 all the graves were removed except Williamson's, which, although unmarked, remains to this day in the small triangular patch of rubble-strewn waste ground which stands at the junction of Paradise Street and Park Lane. Yet who of all the throng who pass this anonymous sepulchre knows anything of this remarkable man; who, among the multitudes who tread daily upon the roof of his underworld, has ever heard the name of its creator? Should anyone be interested to see the face and figure of "The King of Edge Hill" he has but to visit the Edge Hill Public Library where hangs a portrait of him. Strange as it may seem in view of the early date of Williamson's demise, there is a photograph of him in existence, too. It was discovered in unusual circumstances together with one which is believed to be that of his wife. A later owner of Williamson's house made this interesting "find" in a kind of cubby-hole beneath the floorboards in the corner of a room on the first floor. In his photograph, Williamson is represented as a man of about 53 years of age. This dates the photograph as having been taken somewhere about the year 1822, which means that

11

it is one of the earliest examples of photographic portraiture extant.

It is interesting to speculate upon the circumstances which led Williamson to deposit those two faded photographs in the secret place in his home where they lay hidden for nearly a hundred years. He was a grouchy sort of creature and his hasty and unreasonable temper was sometimes the cause of he and his wife, Betty, leading something of a cat-and-dog life. Once, after a specially hectic quarrel, he, regretting no doubt the passing of his bachelor days, flung open the door of his wife's aviary and, as the feathered prisoners winged their way to freedom, he exclaimed dramatically: "There! See how the poor little devils like to get free. Many a married man would like to have wings and the doors of wedlock thrown open so that they might fly away and be at rest." But for all that, when in 1822 Betty Williamson died, her widower, in a moment of tenderness, confessed that he was "Sorry to part with the old girl when she did go!" When it was found, the glass of the ornate gilt frame in which the portrait of Betty Williamson was mounted was badly cracked, perhaps by Williamson himself in one of his rages. It is a pathetic possibility that some time after her death, alone and remorseful, he stole quietly upstairs and placed her photograph, together with his own, in the secret ambry beneath the floor.

During the lonely years that followed the death of Betty, Williamson became more and more eccentric. He gave nearly all of his time to his excavations. He is even said to have taken to living in the cellar, and this despite an abundance of luxury in the regions above stairs. His bedroom was reputedly a kind of cave, hollowed out at the back of the cellar, which has been described as "more like the den of a wild beast than the dwelling place of a human being." Never was such a troglodyte—such a veritable cave-man! When he died there was but £40,000 of his vast fortune left; the rest, probably something in the neighbourhood of £100,000, had been swallowed up in his diggings. He had literally dug deep into his capital!

Today, the house in Mason Street (Number 44 it was) is no more. After Williamson's death it served a variety of purposes; first as a private residence, then as a school, storehouse, barracks of the Royal Engineers, machinery store and garage. But the tunnels are still there.

Up to about thirty years ago there were in existence several entrances to the underground galleries. There was a tunnel which opened into a back-garden in Mason Street and it is said that a passage which ran to the adjacent church of St. Mary's, Edge Hill, was accessible also. There is, too, an amusing anecdote concerning an uncharted entrance from the cellar of a shop which stood formerly at the top of the precipitous street known as Paddington and almost opposite St. Mary's Church. Some years ago a man started a bottling business in these premises which were peculiarly suited to his purpose by reason of the fact that they possessed two deep, cool cellars,

12

one below the other, wherein his stock could be conveniently stored. Unfortunately, however, he soon discovered that bottles were mysteriously disappearing from the lower cellar. Needless to say, the man made a thorough examination and, to his surprise, discovered, in a dark and distant corner, a narrow opening which led into a tunnel, wherein reposed the missing bottles—empty!

It may well have been this same shop, then tenanted by a plumber, which, in November 1926, afforded access to the subterranean world to a party of learned members of the Historic Society of Lancashire and Cheshire, who, under the leadership of the late Charles R. Hand, spent a Saturday afternoon field-meeting happily meandering, for more than a mile, through the bowels of the earth. This shop has long since disappeared but I have myself got down into Williamson's tunnels from the garage which stood upon the site of his house. I was also informed by a workman to whom I spoke on the subject, and who had explored some of the tunnels, that an entrance can still be effected from a small opening in the rock wall of one of Stephenson's tunnels on the nearby railway line. "But there's not much point in going into them," my informant added. "You can't explore them very far, they're nearly all blocked or water-logged. Can't think what the old fellow was thinking of," he went on, "wasting all that time and money making them. What's the use of them, thats what I'd like to know?"

What is the use of them? That is the universal query! Williamson's body had scarce grown cold when the *Liverpool Mercury* uttered that reproachful question which has echoed down the years, taken up time and time again with a naïve assumption of originality. "No earthly use can be assigned for these tunnels," they chorus in a unison of condemnation. Yet, suggestions for their employment have not been wanting—albeit, they have not been altogether untainted with facetiousness! Might they not be used, like the famous catacombs of Paris, as the last abode of crumbling mortality? Would they not make excellent storehouses for the reception of stolen goods? Do they not provide safe quarters where illicit distillers might defy the acuity of the Excise, or a band of daring forgers construct an admirably obscure den? But these suggestions are not practical cry the critics; and this is an era in which the practical is held sacrosanct. Everyone measures this or that activity in terms of profitableness. The hobby pure and simple is at a discount. Williamson spent a vast sum of money on his chosen hobby. A waste? Maybe, but thank goodness for the eccentrics who lend the interest of their originality to life. It will be a sad day for us all when such men cease to be. It would be a colourless world indeed, bereft of their imagination and their courage in translating bold imaginings into as boldly conceived a reality; of such is the stuff of genius. Today, we live in an age of mass-production; men, minds and machines are cast all in a pattern from a master-mould of convention. The cult of the common man rides rough-shod where once it was down-trodden.

But all this happened a long, long time ago. A hundred years and more have passed since the once familiar figure of the "King of Edge Hill" walked the highways and byways of his undisputed demesne, and his body has long since crumbled back into the earth in which he loved to dig. But even though no token signifies his last resting place, Joseph Williamson is by no means forgotten. From time to time his shade emerges from that unmarked grave, casting aside the dusty pall the years have woven about him. In 1926, when the party of local antiquarians explored the long-deserted "Kingdom of Saturn" public interest in his doings was revived and the newspapers paramounted his story. In 1937 many of his tunnels were stumbled on, and into, by workmen engaged in clearing an area of ground close to Paddington preparatory to the erection of the blocks of tenement flats, then extant only in the architect's mind, which now raise stony faces of austere modernity from foundations deep in the rock in which his tunnels wind their unknown ways. Again, in 1940, municipal officers inspected portions of his subterranean galleries with a view to their possible use as refuges from the sky-borne death of war. They pronounced them unsuitable. Some years later Williamson's earthy spectre rose once more with the discovery of yet another tunnel, nineteen feet wide and twenty-five feet high, at Elm Grove, where Liverpool City Housing Department had just begun work on the building of a number of new dwellings.

But the public memory is notoriously short and most of the time Joseph Williamson sleeps quietly at the cross-roads.

2. SOLOMON IN ALL HIS GLORY

This is the curious and very human story of old Doctor Solomon whose lonely mausoleum once stood amidst the fields that stretched below the wooded eminence of Mossley Hill, and whose tonic Balm of Gilead became the universal panacea of a forgotten age.

It was somewhere between the years 1791 and 1796 that a young Jewish doctor named Samuel Solomon made his first appearance in Liverpool and settled down to practise medicine in a house at Number 12 Marybone, Tithebarn Street. Young Solomon's career started in a very humble way, but all that was soon to be altered by the Balm of Gilead, which, whatever it may or may not have done to increase the health of suffering humanity, did a great deal to increase the wealth of its inventor, sole bottler and proprietor—Doctor Solomon!

Now Solomon it seems had the wisdom to appreciate that in order to prove efficacious it is in no wise essential that a medicine should taste disagreeable. Acting upon this sound principle, he compounded in his private laboratory a tonic cordial which he patented under the captivating name of Balm of Gilead. There is a touch of genius in that choice of title, for it is a sagacious blending of the scriptural and the superstitious, guaranteed to appeal alike to the sanguine faith of the truly sick and the fractious caprice of the hypochondriac.

The records are silent regarding the exact date of the invention of the Balm, nor are they any more communicative concerning the prescription according to which it was compounded. Actually, Solomon appears to have kept its composition a closely guarded secret, to ensure the preservation of which he went so far as to purchase its several ingredients in different towns throughout the kingdom. Nevertheless rumour has it that its liquid base consisted of fine old French brandy, admixed with quantities of the richest spices and, in view of the phenomenally wide sales which the Balm achieved, one does not feel disposed to contradict rumour in this respect!

By the end of the eighteenth-century the Balm had become exceedingly popular and its fame had, as Solomon advertised, verily "penetrated to the utmost bounds of the habitable globe." No medicine-chest was complete without its flask of Balm and it is said that in the days of the old East India Company, scarcely a single East Indiaman ploughed its water way to the land of the tiger without its consignment of Solomon's Balm of Gilead aboard. Almost before he knew it, Solomon had become the forerunner of our modern pill and ointment kings and not only did he make his indelible mark in the advertising world of his day, but soon found himself amassing a considerable fortune.

Not unnaturally, Doctor Solomon's rapid success stimulated the rancour of many who watched his progress with thin-lipped envy and he suffered somewhat severely at the hands of critics both in and out of the medical profession. He defended himself, however, from all attacks with a vigour which did him credit, and published a small book entitled *A Guide to Health*, a copy of the undated 66th edition of which is preserved in Liverpool's Picton Library. This book is, not without a certain justification, referred to somewhat scathingly by Watt in his *Bibliotheca Brittannica*, 1824, as "a thing of shreds and patches from the author's own advertisements and Aristotle's masterpiece."

But what did Solomon care for the loud howls of the less fortunate who snapped jealous jaws about his well-shod heels? The shekels were rolling in and everywhere delighted patients were looking forward to having the Balm prescribed as the magic antidote to their multifarious ills. By 1800, the sum of all their half-guineas (the price of a bottle of the Balm, or if you preferred it, a small economy might be achieved by purchasing the 33/- Family Bottle in which was contained the quantity of four normal bottles!) had enabled him to move into a large, newly-erected house, surrounded by a pleasant garden, at the Dansie Street corner of Brownlow Street.

It was in the year 1803, during the period of his residence in Brownlow Street, that Doctor Solomon invested some of his new-found wealth in what was one of the earliest attempts to supply the provinces with a daily newspaper—the *Mercantile Gazette and Liverpool and Manchester Advertiser*, the first number of which was issued on August 6th, 1803. The venture was not a success.

Sped upwards in the wake of his empiric comet, Solomon built himself in 1804 an imposing country mansion in Kensington Fields, whither he removed during the early part of 1805. This place, perhaps out of gratitude to the past, or maybe with an advertiser's eye to the future, he named "Gilead House." It was a large, square, brick edifice, pierced by a series of long windows, each containing the then usual number of twelve panes of glass, and entered through a fine doorway provided with a semi-circular portico supported by splendid Ionic columns. It stood on the north side of the old road to Prescot—then known as Prescot Lane and renamed Kensington about 1804.

Solomon, like his ancient namesake, loved his garden, and the ample grounds which surrounded Gilead House with their beautiful shrubberies, flower-strewn parterres, perfumed rose-gardens and smooth-shaven, emerald-green lawns, attracted many visitors on Sunday afternoons and long summer evenings, being considered at that time one of the sights of Liverpool. For many years it was the first sizeable house as you approached Liverpool from the east, and the sight and smell of its elegant pleasances brought welcome refreshment to the jaded senses of the travellers coming in on the dusty London coach.

Here Solomon lived in royal style and his hospitality became a time-honoured tradition, although it must be admitted that, in common with many self-made men, the doctor showed a distinct partiality in his invitations for the "best people." He courted the society of the top set with a will, nor was he averse to paying handsomely for the indulgence of this little peculiarity! Yet withal, he seems to have been a generous and kindly man and we may set off against this regrettable tendency to snobbishness the inherent goodness of heart which prompted him to give some much-needed land for the building of the Wesleyan Chapel in Moss Street.

His social exuberance knew no bounds and such was the length of his purse that no economic considerations arose perforce to temper his inclinations. A slight contretemps took place at one of these "At Homes." One night Solomon entertained a party of gentlemen to dinner at Gilead House and towards the close of the evening a wag, wishing to draw the doctor, began to bait him about his Balm of Gilead. He took it all in good part and upon being told that he really ought to let those present taste the miraculous fluid, he immediately ordered the servant to bring in some bottles of his patent *elixir vitæ*. These were eagerly sampled and pronounced to be far more palatable than any of the delectable wines with which he had hitherto regaled them. At the end of the evening, just as the guests were preparing to depart, in response to a signal from the doctor, a servant appeared bearing upon a silver salver a quantity of small envelopes. These were distributed among the guests who, upon opening them, discovered that each contained a bill amounting to one guinea in respect of the amount of Balm which they had consumed. Surprised and indignant, a guest inquired disdainfully if he required paying for his hospitality. The doctor replied good-humouredly that he would never dream of it: he freely gave it, but his Balm of Gilead he always sold, adding that it was by means of the Balm that he lived and through it he was enabled to invite them to partake of his hospitality. Each guest paid his bill, admitting that the doctor was right and that they had merited the reproof which their bad taste had caused to be so properly and so promptly administered to them!

As with people, so with possessions, Solomon was satisfied with nothing less than the best. Now it so happened that Lord Sefton boasted a particularly fine four-in-hand in which he would frequently drive past Gilead House on his way to town. It was not long before Solomon decided that he too must have one, and not a whit less elegant that His Lordship's. Thereafter, a distinguished-looking man in a broad-rimmed hat might be seen every day driving his magnificent carriage and four down London Road. It was the doctor's greatest delight to lie in wait for Sefton's carriage and then shadow him townwards in his own. One day both pulled up outside

Heywood's Bank, His Lordship, who was a first-rate whip, in his usual dashing style, and the inexpert Solomon, determined not to be outdone, gave his whip such a tremendous flourish as to lassoo himself about his neck with the lash. The passers-by were amazed by the spectacle of the poor doctor wrestling with his own whip-lash and extremely amused when at last he had to be extricated from its leathern embrace by his groom.

An amusing incident which occurred at Gilead House was occasioned by the visit of Madame Tussaud, who, having recently acquired the relics of Napoleon, had decided that she would also like to add the effigy of this Liverpool Emperor of Empirics to her waxwork gallery of celebrities. The doctor, his vanity tickled, agreed to this proposal and invited her forthwith to Gilead House in order to make a cast of his features. The subject was placed upon his back and Madame Tussaud proceeded to mould the wax upon his face. Unfortunately, however, she forgot to leave any airholes over his mouth and nose. Solomon bore the slow suffocation for a short time, then leaped up in some alarm, tore off the mask and hurled it the length of the room, at the same time shouting angrily, "By God, madam, do you wish to stifle me?" Nor would anything that Madame could say induce him to submit himself again to the preliminary operations of her plastic art.

Incidentally, the doctor took a lively interest in the outcome of the great election of 1818 in which he supported Lord Sefton. At a reputed cost of something like £1,000, he flooded the town with banners and ribbons flaunting his Lordship's colours; addressed, and circulated widely, an eloquent appeal to the electors and played an active part in the campaigning. It is a matter of history that all Solomon's efforts were of no avail, for after a seven days' poll the result was declared:

Canning	. .	1,654
Gascoigne	. .	1,444
Sefton	. .	1,280

Indisputably, Solomon was a clever and original, if somewhat eccentric, man. His politics were Tory but there was much of the Liberal in his mode of life. Although he was Jewish, he never occupied a seat at the Synagogue and, whilst he was indifferent to Jewish practices, it must by no means be assumed that he was devoid of racial sympathies. Indeed, he was the first to come forward with an unsolicited donation of ten guineas when the Jewish community was engaged in the collection of money for the completion of a new Synagogue in Seel Street in 1807. But, realising that neither he nor his family could claim any congregational privileges from the Hebrew community, he gave his children an education far beyond the average of his generation and, likewise aware that he had no reservation of rights in respect of the congregational burial-ground, he decided to build his own mausoleum upon an estate which he owned at Mossley Hill. Thus, what may at first sight appear as a mere folly, takes on when one is in full possession of the facts a very different aspect.

This mausoleum was a costly monument of fine, white sandstone. It was provided with several doors and surmounted by a small, conical obelisk, surrounded by four cone-shaped pinnacles. It stood at one side of a railed enclosure. According to Sheriff's map of 1816, it was situated in a field by the edge of a stream (known as Solomon's Brook) which formed part of the Allerton-Garston boundary. Close by this brook there ran a small footpath which came to be known locally as Solomon's Vaults. It has long since been swept away and the trim, pebble-dashed villas of Cooper Avenue now occupy its site.

The first interment in this mausoleum took place when Solomon's twenty-one-year-old daughter, Sophia (who had married a Mr. Samuel Tobias of London on August 22nd, 1810) died on 2nd June, 1813. On 14th March, 1815, his wife, Elizabeth, died at Gilead House in her fiftieth year, and she too was laid to rest in the mausoleum. The doctor married again, a Miss Jane Martin at Walton Church on 19th June, 1815. Hers was the third body to be buried in the Mossley Hill vault. She died, aged 38, on 13th December, 1818. The doctor himself died, at the age of fifty, whilst on a visit to Bath, on 21st May, 1819, and his body was brought back to Liverpool and placed in his mausoleum. Nor is this dreadful catalogue of deaths yet complete, for there was still one more of Solomon's children who was to be carried into the last fastness of his sandstone deadhouse. On November 17th, 1824, sixteen-year-old Sarah Solomon was borne thither and the mausoleum had claimed its last tenant.

There remained only a son and two daughters. The beautiful Marie married Doctor James Byron Bradley of Buxton and their daughter married the Honourable Mr. Byron. The son of this marriage was the late Henry J. Byron, the well-known author and dramatist, one-time lessee of the old Alexandra Theatre in Lime Street. Solomon's other surviving daughter, Eliza, married George Bradnock Stubbs and bore him a daughter, Emily Eliza, who became the wife of the Reverend Henry J. Newbolt and mother of two great literary and legal figures, Sir Henry and Sir Francis Newbolt. Solomon's only son John, entered the legal profession but, being of independent means, never practised. He was a keen sportsman and prided himself on his prowess as a pugilist. It was his proudest boast that once in his youth he had boxed with Lord Byron. In the early 'forties of the last century, he was a familiar figure crossing the river in pink and pigskin to attend a meet of the Cheshire or Shropshire Hounds. He died, unmarried, at Southport about 1880.

Upon the shortening of the London & North-Western Railway Company's line to the south, via Runcorn, they purchased the field in which the mausoleum stood from Solomon's representatives, and in 1840 it was taken down. The bodies were transferred to the Necropolis (now Grant Gardens, West Derby Road), on September 11th, 1840, where, up to the time of the demolition of the Necropolis in 1912, a perfectly plain slab (Number 4832) without any inscription whatsoever marked the vault in the centre of the main walk where the doctor and his family lay buried.

Nothing of the old Mossley Hill mausoleum now remains. Until a few years ago, there was a broken sculptured slab half buried in the ground in a plantation behind Holmefield House (demolished in 1942) and a few pieces of carved white sandstone lay in a nearby garden. Gilead House was pulled down in 1846 and the land sold for building purposes. Portions of the white Ionic columns, capitals and stone pediment, which once formed its portico, lay for many years, like so many fragments of ruined Greece, on the edge of a stretch of waste land opposite the end of Cottenham Street on the site of the present Kensington Gardens. The glorious grounds which gladdened the hearts of dead generations are now covered by a colony of indistinguished houses, ranged in drab streets named after dusty legal luminaries of the past—Coleridge, Cottenham, Denman, Farnworth, Keble and Seldon. Close by stand Solomon, Balm and Gilead Streets which were erected in 1864-5 opposite the site of Gilead House and so named to do honour to the memory of the illustrious doctor and his fortunate invention.

But dull suburban streets are a poor memorial and perhaps that end is more happily achieved by the anonymous rhymer who wrote:—

Great Solomn has gone,
His home and sepulchre and Balm,
If his mixture did mankind no good,
At least it did no harm.

So, at last, the man who took such pains to raise a fitting monument to commemorate himself is, ironically, unremembered. Somewhere in the story of Samuel Solomon there is, one suspects, a moral concerning the futility of wordly ambition. Throughout life we strive to fashion our carefully-contrived imaginary strongholds, we die and time tears them down. One cannot even be certain now as to the precise location of the unmarked grave wherein the doctor's body lies. But perhaps that does nor really matter, for, after all, it is not the cold clay shell that we shall wish to remember. Perhaps, in some magpie great-grandmother's store-cupboard, is still hidden away a golden bottle of the Balm of Gilead. Rather that we should discover this, and, lifting our glasses, recall the warm generous spirit that was Solomon in all his glory.

3. PORTRAIT OF A LIVERPOOL MUSICIAN

On the night of the fire, a courageous Liverpool gentleman dashed into the flames which licked about the portals of the Green Room and rescued great-grandfather's portrait.

The night in question was that of July 5th, 1933. The fire was the mammoth one which razed the old Philharmonic Hall. And great-grandfather was James Zeugheer-Herrmann, the Liverpool Philharmonic Society's first conductor.

Beyond the fact that he was an intimate of Mendelssohn, what little is known of the early life of this man whose name is so inextricably interwoven with the history of music in Liverpool, can be summed up very briefly.

Born in Zurich, in 1805, of a family of lawyers, he learned the violin from Wasserman in his native city and, when he was thirteen years old, was sent to Munich where he studied under Ferdinand Fränzel (violin) and Gratz (composition). A visit to Vienna in 1823 confirmed an innate enthusiasm for chamber-music and a worship of Beethoven which coloured his whole life.

At the age of nineteen, Herrmann and three friends formed a quartet and, as "Das Quartett Gebrüder Herrmann," they spent the next five years giving concerts all over Europe. They toured Southern Germany and Switzerland and proceeded along the Rhine to Holland, Belgium and France. They crossed the Channel from Bolougne and, in 1826, introduced quartet music into England for the first time.

By the spring of 1830 the "Brothers" had grown weary of this nomadic life and Herrmann decided to settle down in Liverpool. It had been a toss-up between here and London, but his love for the river decided the issue. He ensconced himself at 17 Stafford Street and began to earn his living as a professor of music.

Things went well and, in 1831, he accepted the conductorship of the Gentlemen's Concerts at Manchester. He also did a certain amount of free-lance conducting and it was an orchestra under his direction which accompanied Paganini, the demon fiddler, when he visited Liverpool. Before the concert, Herrmann was summoned to the old Adelphi Hotel. The Italian virtuoso was in bed and all that could be seen of him was a huge nose poking over the bed-clothes. After a short conversation Paganini said, "Ha! I see you understand the score perfectly." And great-grandfather was dismissed. In January 1840, the Liverpool Philharmonic Society, originally a private body, began to give public concerts and three years later Herrmann was appointed its first regular conductor.

At some date concerning which family records are silent, Herrmann had met and married a Miss Anna Barrington of Dublin and, round about

1840, he and his wife moved into 121 Islington. Here they remained for a decade until the demands of a family of seventeen children necessitated their removal to somewhat larger premises at 36 Bedford Street.

It would seem that it was Herrmann's ambition to have his own domestic orchestra for each of the children was taught to play at least one instrument. Some, indeed, played several and one boy was able to perform on no less than twenty-one. Even my grandfather, Alphonse, then only a tiny mite of six, was hoisted onto a little stool and had to play on a specially-made miniature cello! The chidren would practise all over the house and so good was their father's ear that, standing in his dressing-room, he could pick out and name any wrong notes in the resultant cacophony. He would then roar out at the offending musician. Every Friday there was a musical evening and the trembling children used to give a little concert before invited friends, many of whom were eminent in the world of music.

Some years ago I paid a visit to the old house in Bedford Street. It was then owned by the Bedford Stores and used for storage purposes. Standing there amidst the neatly stacked packages of groceries, I tried to fill its bare rooms with something of the warmth of the past. It was while I was in the room which I am sure was once the drawing-room that I found my mind recalling tales of old-time Christmas festivities which were once celebrated within those walls. Great-grandfather had all of the German veneration for *Weinachten* and each December a huge Christmas tree of the kind which never drops its needles was sent from Germany. It used to be decorated with real fruit and was kept in a locked room until the great day arrived. Every year Pappa Herrmann would dress up as Santa Claus. Late on Christmas Eve there would come a thunderous knock on the door and Father Christmas, accompanied by his drunken servant, Tom, would appear leading a live donkey, complete with panniers, right into the basement kitchen. He would then go upstairs to the study where he would call the chidren to him one by one. Producing a mirror, he would look into it and tell them in turn of their outstanding faults during the past year. After that, he would descend to the servants' quarters and drink beer with Drunken Tom. The children were all terrified by this annual apparition and Mary Brian, the superstitious Irish cook, would quake with the best of them! The whole ceremony was brilliantly acted and none of the little ones ever suspected that it was pappa. After more than a century, the identity of Drunken Tom remains a family mystery.

Herrman's working day was a heavy one. It started at 6 a.m. when a carriage would come for him and he would drive all over Liverpool giving tuition. He would have lunch at one or other or his pupil's houses and then carry on teaching until evening. Apart from an extensive round of teaching, he had also to fit in concert rehearsals and often would not get home until late at night. This saddened him, for it was his great delight to play games, such as chess, draughts and halma, with his children.

Actually, Pappa Herrmann was very devoted to his family and might be seen any Sunday setting out proudly with his wife at the rear of a mighty crocodile of their offspring which would wend its way sedately to church. Himself brought up exceedingly strictly, it was his tragedy in life that his children feared him. A sick, worried and overworked man, he could never understand that his apparent harshness frightened them and he often bewailed the fact that they seemed afraid of him.

His severity of manner and Teutonic thoroughness also made Herrmann vaguely unpopular with the Philharmonic Orchestra. A man who never hesitated to drive himself, it may be that he wielded his baton too much like a whip. On one occasion, in 1849, when, at the end of a very long rehearsal Herrmann had harangued them because they were not playing the finish of the then unhackneyed *William Tell Overture* at a sufficiently rapid tempo, the exhausted orchestra decided to have its revenge. When the night of the concert arrived, Blagrove, one of the leaders, whispered to Tom Harper, the renowned trumpet, "How quick can you go, Tom?" "As quick as you like," replied Harper and forthwith proceeded to do so. Indeed, such was the final velocity of that overture that a dismayed Herrmann was left waving his laggard stick helplessly in the air!

By 1864 Herrmann's health was failing. He suffered from a bad heart and the long years of grinding work had taken their toll. On March 28th, 1865, he laid down his baton for the last time and by June 15th he was dead.

They buried him in the old Necropolis but his grave was swept away in 1912 when that ancient burial-place was filled in.

What remains of him today? A handful of songs, waltzes and glees. Before me on my desk lies the score of his opera, *Angela of Venice*. It is contained in two leather-bound volumes and is beautifully written in the neatest and tiniest of manuscript. This work was never published or produced owing to the poorness of Chorley's libretto. There is also, at the new Philharmonic, that old portrait which was salvaged by the late Mr. Percy Ashlyn Hughes on the night of the fire.

Finally, there is a brass inkstand, presented to great-grandfather by Jenny Lind, the Swedish Nightingdale, into which I now dip my pen to write the word . . . FINIS.

4. SHERLOCK HOLMES AND LIVERPOOL

Whether or not Sherlock Holmes was ever in Liverpool is a moot point. Unfortunately, it is one of those many little details concerning which the good Watson is unpardonably vague. Nevertheless, in view of Holmes's extensive travels, we may, I think, take it as reasonably certain that at some time or other in the course of his long and active life the tall, gaunt figure of the world's most famous detective might have been seen moving against some familiar Liverpool background.

Perhaps it would be upon a morning of bright spring sunshine that we should encounter Holmes and Watson strolling down Bold Street towards the heart of the town. Or we might have glimpsed them moving, swift and silent as shadows, beneath the yellow gaslamps of the old landing-stage, fighting a savage winter wind that ruffled the dark waters of the Mersey, as they hurried towards the lowered gangway of the rolling ship aboard which some criminal was about to make his escape. Unexpectedly, they might have emerged from a patch of ground-nestling mist in Sefton park so early upon a November morning that the weak sun's rays had not yet strength enough to drink the dew. They would, perhaps have been heading for the darkly-wooded roads of the older part of Mossley Hill, where, behind the sturdy sandstone wall of some merchant prince's house, the trail of mystery was to reach its tragic end. Maybe they lurked within the shadows when the hunter's moon raised its golden globe above the craggy masses of the Calderstones, awaiting the arrival of dark forces that would come to set their seal upon a compact of evil beside that brooding circle. In drab alleyways in the foreign quarters of our city, where secret dens of opium and what other nameless vices abound, there, too, may Holmes and Watson have prowled through the small hours, when honest citizens are abed and only the partisans of law and lawlessness walk abroad in their respective rôles. Fantasy? Perhaps! But who shall say these things were not?

In any event, Liverpool is certainly mentioned in the chronicles of Dr. Watson, and in his account of Holmes's investigations in the case of *The Cardboard Box* (which appears in the volume of memoirs entitled *His Last Bow*) he quotes Holmes as saying, "I therefore sent off a telegram to my friend Algar, of the Liverpool Force." And if the purist be dissatisfied and persists that I have not made out my case for the association of Sherlock Holmes and Liverpool, let me then offer the self-justification that we in Liverpool are no less interested in, no less erudite concerning, and no less fascinated by, the life and personality of Mr. Sherlock Holmes than are the citizens of any other great city. It is bearing these circumstances in mind that I have permitted myself the present excursion into the changeless world of Conan Doyle's creation.

From Liverpool, then, we must move for a while to London . . .

It is an afternoon towards the end of the nineteenth-century, and the wraiths of a thick, yellow fog twist shapelessly through the muffled mysteriousness of London streets. Although it is but a few minutes since a battlion of silver-tongued clocks have chimed the hour of four, and the smell of hot, buttered crumpets clings about the heavy fold of myriad plush curtains, the gas-lamps are alight and evening is advancing with a cosiness which the age of tubular electricity has already lost.

Upon this afternoon, two men are sitting in the snugness of a first-floor apartment in Baker Street. The room is warm and comfortable and filled with the lesser, aromatic mist of tobacco smoke. One of these men, gaunt and sharp-eyed, is wrapped in a long, purple dressing-gown, and is curiously curled in the depths of a large, shabby armchair. His head is sunk upon his breast and so motionlessly does he sit that you might almost imagine him to be asleep. Actually, he is busily engaged with a powerful magnifying glass in deciphering the remains of an obscure palimpsest. His companion, middle-sized, thickset, liberally moustached and typically English, is deep in some long-forgotten nautical novel of Clarke Russell's and has about him an air of satisfied mediocrity as he stretches his legs to the sea-coal glow within the hearth. Outside, the darkness and the fog deepen and a drizzle of rain begins to fall. The rank shag burns low in the black bowls of their pipes and within the room the men stir as their ears catch the first sharp echoes of a hansom moving through the empty, shining street, bearing yet another singular adventure to the doorstep of Mr. Sherlock Holmes and the ever-faithful Doctor Watson.

It is a charming domestic vignette to set against those moments of high drama and frantic activity when Holmes, transformed into a feelingless human bloodhound, remorselessly hunts the luckless wrong-doer to his destruction; a picture which will endure with all the timeless tenacity of those things which have no existence outside that beloved make-believe world of the mind where it is always an afternoon towards the end of the nineteenth-century.

But time will not stand still, even in the country of the imagination, and at last it must be sadly admitted that both the actors in these perennially re-enacted dramas of more than half a century ago, are dead. I have before me as I write the yellowing fragment of Holmes's obituary. From this it would appear that Sherlock Holmes died in Sussex in November 1948, in his 93rd year. The detective's declining years were spent in peaceful retirement, from which he emerged briefly to solve the mystery of the death of the late Mr. Fitzroy McPherson, who was found dead at the stone feet of the Seven Sisters in July 1907. Although much mystified at first, Holmes eventually succeeded in solving this case when he recollected a passage from his omnivorous reading—*Medusa and Her Locks* from *Out of Doors* by that grand old Victorian pioneer of popular natural history, the Reverend J. G. Wood—which led him to the correct conclusion that the fearful jellyfish, *Cyanea capillata*, was the assassin. He lived with a housekeeper to look after him at a small farmhouse on the Downs, some five miles from Eastbourne, and devoted the greater part of his time to his hobby of beekeeping, the reading of philosophy, the study of dew-ponds and the collection of chalk fossils. He was surprisingly active to the last, although subject to periodic attacks of rheumatism.

But we will not waste time and sympathy upon considerations of Holmes's death, for he, who had no life, is assured of survival long after we, his mourners, are unremembered dust. Nor shall we dwell upon the silver years of his decline. Let us rather recall him in those urgent, vital days when the yellow sunlight grilled the bricks of Baker Street and he and Watson sat behind the half-drawn blinds until some strange turn of events would send them speeding in hansom through breathless August streets.

It was upon just such a day that a paragraph in the *Daily Chronicle* directed their attention to the reception by a harmless maiden lady in Croydon of a small cardboard box containing a couple of freshly-severed human ears. Of course it was not long before Lestrade of the Yard was enlisting the aid of his friend in Baker Street. Step by step, Holmes picked his way through the maze of mystery until at length he was able to disclose that, what had at first sight appeared to everyone as nothing more serious than the mischievous prank of some medical student possessed of a dissecting-room brand of humour, was in reality the grisly evidence of a double murder. This particular adventure *(The Cardboard Box)* is of special interest to us, as the events leading up to the arrival of the gruesome packet were set against a Merseyside background. Holmes's uncanny powers enabled him, without ever leaving London, to uncover a drama of love and hate, staged in the small house in Liverpool that was the home of seafaring Jim Browner and his wife, Mary. Within a matter of hours, Holmes is able to supply Lestrade with the murderer's name. A bewildered Jim Browner is subsequently arrested and breaks down and confesses everything. His confession reveals the whole tragic story of how, enraged by jealousy of his wife's lover, he followed them on an occasion when they, imagining him to be away at sea, had decided to take a trip to New Brighton. The day was hot and the lovers hired a boat in order that they might be alone together on the river. But Browner, who was close behind them, followed in another boat and all three were soon hidden from prying eyes behind a curtain of haze. Browner overtook them and killed first the man who was responsible for the ruin of his marriage, and then his wife. He severed an ear from each body, tied them together, and then stove in the bottom of the boat, which

26

sank with its gruesome burden to the bed of the Mersey.

It is equally pleasant to recall the two friends upon a sharp morning of winter frost, when the newly-kindled flames leap orange in the grate, and the breakfast-table china winks whitely in the bright light as Holmes pores over the agony column of *The Times,* smoking the dottle chargings of his matutinal pipe. Perhaps a strangely worded insertion will play its jigsaw part in the all-important quest that is afoot, or, maybe, a distant bell will ring, and ponderous, puffing Mrs. Hudson will usher in some fresh and human facet of a mystery. The setting are various, but there is always a certain indefinable sense of momentousness about the slightest details of the commencement of an investigation. Not only Holmes, but we also, should be grateful for the felicitous pen of Watson, which has, perhaps by very reason of its frequent delineation of the apparently trivial and inconsequent, done so much to preserve the essence of the spirit which animated the wondering chronicler.

We owe almost all of our knowledge of Sherlock Holmes to the indefatigable Watson, but it is with something of regret that we search his writings vainly for some details of Holmes's earlier life. It may be that Holmes himself was reticent upon these points. Of his birth we know nothing, save the fact that it took place in the year 1855, and that, according to his own account, he came out of country squire stock, into whose blood a strain of artistry was introduced when his grandfather married the sister of Vernet, the French artist. That he spent some time at a university is also certain, since it is recorded in the account of his first case *(The Gloria Scott)* that it was the father of a fellow-student , Victor Trevor, whose guest he was at Donnithorpe in Norfolk, who first advised Holmes to undertake the career in which he was destined to achieve such unchallenged eminence. The sum of the evidence would indicate that he was at Oxford University. The College one feels, with apologies to Lady Bracknell, is immaterial.

In the account of the extraordinary affair of *The Musgrave Ritual*, we are afforded another glimpse of the young Holmes. Now, he has left the university and has established himself in rooms in Montague Street, just around the corner from the British Museum. Here he waits for clients, filling in his time with the pursuit of those out-of-the-way studies which will, in his opinion, fit him the better for his unusual calling. It was, very likely, at this period that he wrote some of those fascinating monographs to which we shall have occasion to refer later. It is at Montague Street that he receives his first commissions. They come mostly through the recommendations of former fellow-students. It is his third investigation—*The Musgrave Ritual*—which brings success. Thereafter he is looking about for more spacious and impressive quarters, but his resources are still pitifully limited. It is at this juncture, while he is also engaged in pursuing a somewhat curious course of studies in the chemical laboratory and dissecting rooms (where he caused some degree of scandal by beating subjects with a stick in order to verify how far bruises may be produced after death) of St. Bartholomew's Hospital, that John H. Watson, M.D., appears upon his horizon and the pair move into those now world-famous rooms at 221b Baker Street.

From now on the doings of Sherlock Holmes are fairly well documented. Even so, there occur in the Watsonian chronicles references to well over fifty cases of which Watson has left no known records. Among these are mentioned at least two cases which I have reason to believe took place in or near Liverpool—*The Adventure of the Tired Captain*, and *The Tarleton Murders*.

It is to the writings of Dr. Watson that we are indebted for our knowledge of Holmes's methods. According to Watson, Holmes always regarded himself as a machine, a machine in which any admission of emotion would take on the significance of a serious flaw in a delicate mechanism. Yet, for all his belief in the necessity of emotional detachment, he had a fine dramatic sense and could seldom resist the temptation to indulge this certain sense of theatre. It has been said with truth that when Holmes turned to detection the stage lost a great actor. He was a master of disguise and could, when the need arose, assume a completely different personality, in which guise he would take up his quarters in one or other of at least five permanent hideouts which he had in London.

The methods of Sherlock Holmes are of considerable importance, for, having made all due allowances for the unique and inimitable personality of the man, which must have accounted in large measure for some of his successes, it is an undeniable fact that the general principles which he laid down for the scientific conduct of criminal investigations have contributed very materially to modern police methods. Indeed, the celebrated Edmund Locarde, late principal of the Laboratory of Police Technique at Lyons, himself a worthy pioneer in the field of scientific criminology, made public acknowledgment of his indebtedness to Sherlock Holmes! Observation and deduction were the two basic principles of Holmes's methods. He had an enormous appetite for the minute. The selective observation of apparantly insignificant trifles led him to cumulative recognition of important generalisations. Tobacco played a major part in his scheme of things, and Watson frequently draws for us the picture of his friend leaning back in his armchair, his eyes half shut, finger-tips pressed together as he sought the answer to some vexing riddle in the acrid blue clouds that gathered about his head. It was characteristic of the man to refer to a particularly difficult piece of reasoning as a "three-pipe problem." Sometimes he would seek clarity or stimulation less harmlessly, and then, shot with morphine or cocaine, he would lie brooding hour after hour watched by the anxious

Watson. In another mood he would turn to music for his inspiration and then the old violin would be drawn lovingly from its case in the corner and high and low its melancholy vibrations would stab thinly and ceaselessly the tranquil air, until the tortured drums of Watson's ears could stand the high tooth-ache-like frequency no longer and he was driven to the quieting anodyne of the streets.

Unfortunately, the collected edition of Homes's works, which was to have been published under the title of *The Whole Art of Detection*, has never made its appearance, and, although he wrote a great deal, his writings have become inexplicably rare. The two case-records which he wrote under the titles of *The Blanched Soldier* and *The Lion's Mane* are still in print and easily obtainable, but the papers and monographs which he produced upon such diverse subjects as tobacco ash, the typewriter in its relation to crime, tatto marks, the surface anatomy of the human ear, the polyphonic motets of Lassus, malingering, and Chaldean roots in the ancient Cornish language, remain the undiscovered desiderata of numberless bibliophiles.

If the recollection of Sherlock Holmes at work is pleasant and exciting to those of us who need have had no fear of his incomparable skill, we must not neglect to consider the occupation of his leisure hours. There were long weeks when he would lie listlessly upon his horsehair sofa, his body inert, but his nimble mind borne upon the strong wings of cocaine through realms of needle fantasy. There were occasional visits to Covent Garden on a Wagner night or to hear the De Reskes in *Les Huguenots*. At the end of a tiring bout of sustained investigation there would be a last minute rush to Hallé's concert to relish the virtuoso bowing of Neruda or the soothing melodies of St. James's Hall. Sometimes it would be a Turkish bath or a pleasant little dinner *à deux* at Simpson's or Marcini's. The acres of the Bond Street picture-galleries were another strong attraction and Holmes and Watson often enjoyed a wander through the streets, gazing into the shop-windows and speculating as to the lives and occupations of the passers-by. Now and again they would stroll together through the long summer twilight in the park, where, to the accompaniment of a proudly militaristic band, the scarlet soldiers, mustachioed and bewhiskered animations of those we see eternally captured in the frozen instant of dead, daguerrotype images, promenaded, all buttons and neat, pill-box hats, with a small, silver-knobbed cane under one arm and a pretty, crinolined companion upon the other.

But it is the picture of them comfortably busy in their own rooms which we like best. Preferably it is a squally winter's night. Watson may be glancing through the latest treatise on surgery or writing up the history of an adventure. It is not one of those evenings when Holmes is intent upon some malodorous chemical experiment which will finally drive a sorely-tried and muttering Watson from the room. Nor is he amusing himself in a flush of royalist fervour by picking out in patriotic bullet-pocks a huge "V.R." upon a virgin expanse of the wall. Presently Holmes will turn to the doctor and, selecting a glowing cinder from the fire, will light his well-coloured calabash. The atmosphere grows mellow. They drink a friendship's glass of whisky-and-soda, spiced with a yellow rind of lemon. The long rows of scrapbooks, collected over the years, catch the fire-gleams on their leather backs; the huge, precarious piles of London dailies are lying about awaiting the burst of energy that will reduce their bulk to cut and pasted orderliness within the scrapbook covers. Soon Holmes will be communicative, it is that kind of night! In the long hours which separate them from their beds he will tell Watson the story of another of his adventures. Perhaps it will be one of those which he will not allow his friend to publish but which will nevertheless be dutifully recorded at some future date and stowed away with all those other untold tales, which, Watson himself assures us, rest, even now, in mildewing isolation within that battered, black tin box somewhere in the vaults of Cox & Co., at Charing Cross. Some day, maybe, that box may come to light, and new generations of Holmes's admirers will read the records of forgotten cases, some at least of which, I have no doubt, will dispel the aura of uncertainty which surrounds much that is mysterious in the crumbling files of Liverpool's past. They will tell of a lost Liverpool, a Liverpool that lives only in the atmosphere that clings about its old buildings and finds its voice only in the eternal moaning of its ships. And so we will leave Holmes and Watson, ageless and secure in their unchanging world. They are the immortals and it is we, the mortals, and our cities who change and pass away.

5. THE NINE-FOOT "CHILDE"

Beneath a flat grey stone in the peaceful graveyard of Hale Church on the outskirts of Liverpool, lies the body of John Middleton the gigantic "Childe" of Hale.

More than three hundred and fifty years have gone by now since, at the age of forty-five, the giant, whose portrait swings creaking in the Mersey wind upon the sign of the nearby village inn, was laid to rest in the shadows of the 500-year-old tower of the church of what Carlyle's wife once called "the beautifullest village in all England." But the "Childe" is still remembered about those parts and, indeed, has passed out of life into legend to become probably the most famous of English giants.

The first person to mention the fantastic John Middleton in literature was, oddly enough, that irrepressible Jacobean tattler and diarist, Samuel Pepys. Writing in his diary for June 9th, 1668, Pepys records: "To Oxford, a very sweet place . . . After come home from the schools, I out with the landlord to Brazen-nose College; to the butteries, and in the cellar to find the hand of the Childe of Hales . . ."

It is to Robert Plott, the first keeper of Oxford's Ashmolean Museum, that posterity is indebted for the most reliable record of the giant's dimensions. "From the carpus to the end of his middle finger," says Plott, "was 17 inches long, his palm 8 inches and a half broad, and his whole height 9 feet 3 inches."

John Middleton, who was born in 1578, was 39 years old before he achieved any real celebrity. In 1617 King James I was visiting Lancashire and he came, on August 20th of that year, to the vicinity of Hale. Here, he paid a visit to Hale Hall, the seat of the Ireland family, in order to create Gilbert Ireland Knight. At that time, Middleton was in Sir Gilbert's service and it is very likely that when "the wisest fool in Christendom," who was famous for his belief in witches and warlocks, heard of this massive man he found in his existence heartening confirmation of a like belief in the existence of gnomes and giants. At any rate, the regal interest was roused, and in the autumn of that same year Sir Gilbert took Middleton to London.

And a wonderful figure the giant must have cut, for, in order that he might do honour to his native county, a number of Lancashire gentlemen saw to it that he was magnificently accoutred with "large ruffs about his neck and hands, a striped doublet of crimson and white; around his waist a blue girdle embroidered with gold; large white plush breeches powdered with blue flowers; green stockings; broad shoes of a light colour, having red heels and tied with large bows of red ribbon; just below his knees bandages of the same colour with large bows; by his side a sword, suspended by a broad belt over his shoulder, and embroidered, as his girdle, with blue and gold, with the addition of gold fringe upon the edge."

Thus gorgeously arrayed, he is said to have had a bout with the King's Wrestler in the course of which he dislocated his thumb "by which awkwardness, he disobliged the courtiers and was sent back, the King giving him £20." This gratuity was considerably smaller than he had expected and to make matters worse as he was returning to Lancashire his comrades robbed him "so that he was oblig'd to follow the plow to his dying day."

On his way home to Hale the "Childe" passed through Oxford and, naturally, Sir Gilbert, who had matriculated at Brasenose in 1578, made a point of exhibiting his protégé to the members of his old college, many of whom were Lancashire men.

It was while the "Childe" was staying at Oxford that an outline of his hand was made on one of the doorposts of a cellar door under the south side of the college hall. This handprint remained, with the addition of a gilt background, until about 1886 and was in all probability the "hand" of which Pepys wrote.

Today, a life-size portrait of John Middleton hangs in the college library. This picture, which had formerly hung for generations in Hale Hall, was presented to Brasenose by Colonel Ireland Blackburne in 1924. It was very likely painted for Sir Gilbert Ireland, though it has been suggested that it is merely a rather poor copy of a very much more pleasing likeness, attributed to the celebrated Belgian portraitist Marcus Gheerhaerts, which is still preserved at High Legh Hall, near Knutsford.

There are also two allegedly life-sized paintings of the "Childe's" hands which have for many years graced the walls of the Brasenose Buttery. Unfortunately, they are, however, of different sizes. That of the right hand measuring 11 inches in length, while that of the left is fully 16 inches. The former is indisputably the older of the two and probably the more honest.

The "Childe" occupies a prominent place among Brasenose traditions, and his name is better known to many college men than that of the college founder. He became associated with the idea of great power and, since 1815, the year of the earliest recorded "Summer Eights" when Brasenose were Head of the River, successive college boats have been called after him.

As might be expected, a crop of legends tall enough to obscure even the gigantic figure of John Middleton grew up about him.

There is a hollow in the sands at Hale, just below where a cliff, whose summit in spring is buttered with daffodil fields, slopes to the river's edge, wherein John Middleton is said to have fallen asleep one day. As he slept, we are informed, he dreamed that he should be the greatest man in England. And when he awoke he began to meditate upon his dream and came to the conclusion that it portended that he would grow to be a very big man in size, whereupon his buttons immediately flew off and he grew there and then into a prodigious giant. The wiseacres afterwards blamed him, saying that if only he had interpreted his dream aright he should have been great in riches and honour for he had been under a spell and should have been great in whatever he imagined. On his way homewards he was attacked by a furious bull but so strong had he become that he seized it by the horns as it charged him and flung it an immense distance. The bull, used to doing the tossing itself, was much afraid and "suffered him to proceed without further molestation."

The "Childe's" strength became a byword and it was said that he was so powerful that in order to restrain him in the deliriums of an illness his friends had perforce to chain him to his sick-bed. When at length he recovered, two of the chains were given away. One was sent to Chester to keep the Dee Mills from floating down the river and the other was sent to Boston, in Lincolnshire, to prevent the Stump from being blown into the sea. The third was lent in order to chain down His Infernal Majesty who had been captured when suffering from an internal complaint!

But apart from the immense strength that went with it, his size alone was awe-inspiring. Tradition tells of some robbers who once tried to break into the cottage where Middleton and his mother lived. They had removed a window and were just about to enter when they were confronted by a figure so huge that it could only stand erect in the centre of the cottage. So terrified were they by what they believed to be an apparition, that with yells of fear they took to their heels and never looked behind them till they reached the shore of the Mersey at Liverpool.

Lest we be tempted to dismiss, too, John Middleton's proportions as the exaggerations of a romantically-inclined age, it must be recorded that, in the spirit of scientific curiosity which animated nineteenth-century investigators, the giant's remains were, in the early 1800's, dug up from the grave in which they had rested since his death in 1623. "The os femoris," writes Matthew Gregson, "were taken up from the earth and were observed to reach from the hip of a man of common size to his foot." That is a distance of roughly 2 feet 9 inches. This masive overgrowth in the length of the thigh-bones indicates an excessive secretion of the growth hormone throughout childhood and adolescence so that the story of the "Childe's" having become a giant in a single afternoon is definitely disposed of by medical evidence. The great size of his hands suggests the complication of acromegaly and everything points to a clinical picture of primary uncomplicated gigantism upon which was super-imposed acromegaly and hyper-normal activity of the pituitary gland. It is interesting to note that a descendant of the "Childe's" family, Charles Chadwick, who was living in 1804, was over 6 feet in height.

The bones, after being kept at Hale Hall for some years, were eventually re-intered in the village churchyard, and barely a hundred yards away, beneath a slate floorstone in the church, slumbers Middleton's benefactor, Sir Gibert Ireland, who died in 1675, the last of his house.

Truly, "There were giants in the earth in those days," and it is undeniably a monstrous strange relic of old mortality that lies hidden below the outsize tombstone which dwarfs its neighbours, even as the man it commemorates made pygmies of his contemporaries, in the green solitude of Hale Chruchyard, where, securely cradled in his earthen bed, slumbers John Middleton, the nine-foot "Childe."

6. QUEEN OF THE WASH-HOUSES

If ever a saint walked the unyielding pavements of this city of Liverpool it was Kitty Wilkinson.

"It is the poor who help the poor," says the old saw, and you could not find better proof of it than in the dedicated life of the heroic little woman who brought so much of light into the dark lives of those about her. But Kitty did more than earn the loving gratitude of the scores of nineteenth-century working-class families to whom she brought relief, for it was her brave example that inspired a valuable social service—the founding in Liverpool of the first public wash-house.

Kitty herself was not a Liverpudlian. She was born, Catherine Seward, in Londonderry in 1786, and was the daughter of an Irish woman and an English soldier. Her father died while she was still a child, leaving his widow the hard task of bring up a family of three young children.

Towards the end of the eighteenth-century, Mrs. Seward, like many another Irish family of the time, decided to quit the Emerald Isle and cross the Irish Sea to Liverpool. It was for her a voyage into tragedy, for the vessel in which she sailed was wrecked. The crew and passengers took to a small boat and Kitty, her brother and mother were saved, but her infant sister was washed out of her mother's arms by a large wave and drowned. The shock of losing her baby permanently affected the young mother and she subsequently lost, first her sight, and later her reason.

Thus, Kitty's childhood was one of dire poverty and distress for her mother, though skilled in spinning and lace-making, was, because of her poor state of health, unable to earn enough money for the adequate support of her children. But little Kitty was blessed with the friendship of an aged blind lady, Mrs. Lightbody, who did a great deal to help the stricken family. She gave Mrs. Seward employment teaching other poor women how to spin and Kitty spent her days in Mrs. Lightbody's house assisting the servants. During this time she learned to read and Mrs. Lightbody, whose regular companion she became, instilled into her young mind the principles of religion and duty. When her mistress was carried out in her sedan chair— she was so lame as to be unable to walk or climb into a carriage—on her round of charitable missions, Kitty always went with her and the child came to love her benefactress very deeply: One day Mrs. Lightbody called the little girl to her and said: "Kitty, poverty will probably be your portion through life, but you will have one talent to exercise; you may be able to read for half an hour to a sick neighbour, or to run an errand for those who have no one else to go for them. Promise me, child, that you will try to do what you can for others, and then we may meet again in another world, where I shall be thankful to see you above me," and there and then she made a vow which was to shape her life thenceforth, that she would devote herself unceasingly to the service of her neighbours.

Shortly after this conversation, Kitty's mother's health became so much worse that she was obliged to go into the Liverpool Infirmary, and upon her discharge from hospital she returned to Ireland so that she might be among friends who would be willing to look after her. Eleven-year-old Kitty and her brother remained in Liverpool and the kindly Mrs. Lightbody, thinking that country air might benefit the two delicate children, arranged for them to go to work in a cotton-mill at Caton, near Lancaster, which was owned by a relative of hers. Kitty was to remain there, supremely happy, for the next seven years, and it was while she was at Caton that Mrs. Lightbody died, leaving a gap in Kitty's young life that was never to be filled.

In 1804 her mother came back to Liverpool, and Kitty determined to leave the mill in order to look after her. Having settled Mrs. Seward in the best lodgings that she could afford, Kitty went into the service of a Colonel Maxwell. The situation was a good one, but a year had hardly elapsed when the Colonel and his wife left Liverpool. They asked Kitty if she would go with them but such was her sense of duty to her ailing parent that she felt obliged to refuse. She soon found another job with the family of Mrs. Richard Heywood, but at the end of three years her mother's health had again deteriorated. This time Kitty decided that she could no longer go on living out, but would have to go to live with Mrs. Seward.

In order to maintain them, Kitty next opened a species of school. She took a large room, for which she had to pay £5 a year rent, and there, at a charge of 3d. a week, she taught reading and sewing to ninety-three pupils. Her mother sat in a corner during the lessons and occupied herself with lace-making and at night, when the school work was over, Kitty used to go out to sell the caps and other things which Mrs. Seward had made.

Somehow or other Kitty contrived to keep her little school going for about five years, but all the time her mother was becoming increasingly violent. Often, she would burn their small store of food, wood and coal and destroy their clothes and bedding, and her ever more frequent bouts of tantrums frightened the children so much that their mothers took them away, and Kitty had at length to close the school down. Briefly, in 1812, it looked as if fortune was going to smile upon the harassed Kitty, for a French sailor, named John De Monte, proposed to her and she accepted him. In 1815 she gave birth to a son, but a little while after, when she was bearing a second child, she learned that her husband had been lost at sea.

After that, things became pretty desperate. Kitty had to go out charring and working in the fields. She would rise at 2 o'clock in the morning and tramp the roads in search of manure to sell. Despite all this, for forty-eight hours before the birth of her second son, she and her mother had no food other than one penny bread roll.

Her recovery from this confinement was long and tedious, but as soon as she was strong enough she went out to work in a nail-factory. They paid her 3d. for every 1,200 nails she made and her average weekly wage amounted to 4s. To make matters worse, her fingers got badly burned by the hot nails and eventually became so terribly blistered and inflamed that in twelve months she had to give the work up.

Then it was charring and doing odd jobs in the fields again until she was befriended by the wife of a Mr. Alexander Braik, a dyer who lived in Pitt Street. During the last eighteen months of her life this lady suffered a most painful illness and Kitty was constantly occupied in nursing her. When Mrs. Braik died, her husband presented Kitty with a mangle and she began to take in washing.

Now, she toiled more laborously than ever, sometimes twenty-three hours out of the twenty-four, and with nothing more substantial than a bowl of thin water-gruel to sustain her at the end of it. And throughout all this grinding poverty she never once complained and, indeed, was ever willing to help those who were in need with gifts of food or even a few pence when she had them. "Nobody was ever the poorer for what they gave to a neighbour in distress," she would say with a smile.

Kitty remarried in 1823. Her second husband was Thomas Wilkinson, who had been an apprentice in the cotton-mill where she had worked at Caton. The story goes that Wilkinson, having come to Liverpool to earn a living as a porter in Mr. Rathbone's cotton warehouse, was walking one day through the grimy Liverpool streets when he heard someone singing one of the old Lancashire songs that he knew so well. Listening intently, he seemed to recognise the voice of the singer, and it was in this way that he met again, after so many years, the girl he had loved and lost at Caton. Of course they were married and spent nearly a quarter of a century together in the most perfect harmony.

At this time Kitty was living in Denison Street, in one of those cellar-dwellings in which the poor commonly lived in those bitter days. During the years succeeding their marriage, the Wilkinson home became a refuge for all sorts of unwanted children and aged folk who had none to care for them. Kitty shouldered such burdens without a thought, and how she managed is a complete mystery—a small miracle maybe.

At one period this remarkable little woman was keeping a family of fourteen on £2-4-6d. a week and, however much the pound sterling may have decreased in value since Kitty Wilkinson's day, £2-4-6d., 10s. 6d. of which went in rent and water, was even then an absurdly small sum with which to face such commitments. Yet for all its lack of luxuries, the Wilkinson household was a happy and cultivated one, where ample, if plain, meals were provided, and the long evenings passed in playing games, listening to music and reading aloud. A home which, humble though it was, attracted the regular visits of teachers from the Liverpool Mechanics' Institute.

Thus far, Kitty had already lived a truly saintly life of selfless devotion to others, but it was in 1832, when the dreadful cholera epidemic broke out in Liverpool, that she was to do her most heroic work. Day and night, this courageous woman flitted in and out of the houses of the sick and dying. She became the ministering angel of the epidemic and, apart from fearlessly nursing the sick and helping the overworked doctors, she made every morning sufficient porridge to feed sixty poeple, and gave up her very bedroom so that twenty children whose parents had the fever might be washed and tended there. She contributed sheets and blankets for sick-beds from her own slender stock, and placed her tiny kitchen, which contained a boiler, at the disposal of her neighbours so that they might wash and disinfect with chloride of lime those disease-laden clothes and bedding which their poverty-stricken owners could not afford to lose. It was in this kitchen of hers that the idea of a public wash-house first originated.

Fourteen years after the cholera outbreak, a public baths and wash-house was opened in Frederick Street and Kitty and her husband were appointed as its first superintendents.

Nor was all that she had done so quietly during the time of the cholera to go unrecognised, for it had come to the ears of some important personages. One day Kitty was summond to Carnatic Hall where she found many people gathered to do her honour and the Lady Mayoress presented her with a silver tea-service. On the teapot was inscribed:

"The Queen, the Queen Dowager, and the
Ladies of Liverpool
to Catherine Wilkinson, 1846."

But even in the long-delayed moment of her triumph, Kitty was not to know complete happiness, for within a very short space of time Thomas Wilkinson was dead.

Kitty lived on for more than twelve years after his death. For four years the widow and her son looked after the Frederick Street Wash-house, until, in 1852-3, it was pulled down in order to erect a larger and better equipped wash-house upon its site. Mrs. Wilkinson was "compensated" for the loss of her job by being allowed to make and hem all the towels for the new establishment at a salary of 12s. a week! Fortunately, some of the "Ladies of Liverpool" collected among themselves enough money to purchase a small annuity for her.

She died, aged 73, on November 11th, 1860. Her memory, and that of "all poor helpers of the poor," was perpetuated in the Staircase Window of the Lady Chapel of Liverpool Cathedral. Kitty herself is buried a few hundred yards away in St. James's Cemetery. And surely she rests content in the knowledge that she did most wonderfully keep that childhood vow to her beloved friend Mrs. Lightbody. And every now and then a few simple flowers, carefully arranged in empty milk bottles, are placed upon her grave, doubtless the grateful tribute of the poor who still remember their gallant little champion and friend—Catherine of Liverpool.

7. THE ARMLESS MIDGET WHO PAINTED KINGS

Thirty-seven inches in height, possessed of neither hands nor arms, Sarah Biffin would not seem exactly fitted by nature to follow the profession of an artist.

And yet this pathetically handicapped little fragment of humanity had her work hung at the Royal Academy, was awarded the Society of Art's medal, and enjoyed the patronage of four reigning monarchs.

For sheer guts and courage in the face of overwhelming physical disabilities, those of us who are blessed with normal bodies and health and strength must give ungrudging admiration to one of the quaintest little creatures ever to be called a woman. She lies buried in St. James's Cemetery, for it was here in Liverpool that she spent the last years of her life.

The daughter of humble, though normal, parents, Sarah Biffin was born at East Quantoxhead, near Bridgewater in Somerset, on October 25th, 1784. A sensitive and independent-natured little girl, Sarah managed at an early age to acquire an amazing skill with the aid of her mouth and shoulders.

She learned to use scissors, became an expert needlewoman and, while still in her 'teens, contrived to cut out and make all her own clothes.

There also developed in Sarah Biffin a deep and abiding passion for art, and when an artist named Dukes offered to give her lessons in painting she readily accepted.

In return, she had to put herself entirely in Mr. Dukes's charge and was to travel about the country with him exhibiting herself and her achievements at rural fairs. Accordingly, an agreement was drawn up binding her to Mr. Dukes for a period of sixteen years and Sarah Biffin began her career as a fairground freak.

A large booth was hired for her and notices were printed announcing that Mr. Dukes would pay the sum of one thousand guineas to anyone who could show that the armless wonder did not do all that was claimed.

So, she took her place along with the fat woman, the human skeleton, the pig-faced lady and the smallest man on earth and, at a cost of one shilling for a place in the pit, or alternatively, sixpence for a seat in the gallery, the crowds flocked to gaze at Sarah and watch while she wrote her autograph, drew exquisite landscapes or painted dainty little miniatures on ivory. These latter, by the way, could be purchased for three guineas.

It is a sad comment upon human nature that, despite the large amount of money which she earned for him, at no time did Sarah receive more than £5 a year from Mr. Dukes.

It was while exhibiting herself at one of the Race Week fairs that Sarah was first seen by the Earl of Morton, and from that moment the little artist's success was assured. The earl was so impressed by her skill and courage that he commissioned her to paint his portrait. Delighted with the result, he showed it to George III and secured for her the King's favour.

Thereafter the earl made several attempts to rescue his protégé from Mr. Dukes's clutches, but, despite his liberal offers of compensation, Dukes refused to relinquish his claim on Miss Biffin, and she, though not legally obliged to do so, stuck faithfully to the terms of their agreement.

To Dukes, Sarah was merely a dwarf freak who could use a paintbrush, but the earl saw her as a talented artist and arranged for her to receive instructions from W. M. Craig, one of the finest miniature-painters of his day.

When the sixteen years were up, Sarah left the employ of Mr. Dukes, and rapidly improved her painting technique under Craig's tuition. That was the heyday of eighteenth-century miniature-painting, graced by the work of such men as Craig and Cosway, and to the names of these famous artists was soon to be added that of Sarah Biffin.

After she had received a medal from the Society of Arts in 1821, Sarah became a fashionable rage.

During the succeeding years she was patronised by George III, George IV, William IV, Queen Victoria, and many other illustrious and distinguished personages, including the King of Holland, to whom she was appointed miniature-painter.

She held numerous exhibitions of her work all over England—among them, one in the Liverpool Collegiate Institution in Shaw Street, and another in what was then the Liverpool Mechanics' Institute.

By now she was able to support herself entirely from the proceeds of her art, and this was undoubtedly the happiest period of her life.

In 1824 she married a Mr. Wright, but unfortunately he turned out to be Mr. Wrong as far as she was concerned and they never lived together.

There was a rumour later that Wright received a very large sum of money from her at the time of their marriage and that he appropriated it and deserted her. Sarah herself contracted that, however, and she said that for as long as he could manage to do so her husband generously allowed her £40 a year out of a very moderate salary.

During the '30's and '40's of the last century, when Charles Dickens was writing, Sarah Biffin was at the height of her fame and, like many another feature of the contemporary scene, she found her way into the pages of his immortal novels.

If you turn to Chapter Thirty-seven of *Nicholas Nickleby* you will find the following classic reference by Mrs. Nickleby to the gentleman in the next house:

"The Prince Regent was proud of his legs, and so was Daniel Lambert; he was proud of his legs. So was Miss Biffin; she was—no," added Mrs. Nickleby correcting herself, "I think she had only toes, but the principle's

the same. "

From the foregoing extract it will be seen that Dickens shared with a great many other people the popular confusion which existed regarding Miss Biffin's legs. In Chapter Twenty-eight of *Martin Chuzzlewit* he further complicates the issue when he makes Mr. Pip repeat what the Viscount had said to him:

"There's a lot of feet in Shakespeare's verse, but there ain't any legs worth mentioning in Shakespeare's plays, are there, Pip? Juliet, Desdemona, Lady Macbeth, and all the rest of 'em, whatever their names are, might as well have no legs at all, for anything the audience know about it, Pip. Why, in that respect they are all Miss Biffins to the audience, Pip!"

Even the *Dictionary of National Biography* deprives Miss Biffin of legs! The whole vexed question was ventilated many years ago in *Chambers's Journal*, where a writer definitely stated that the lady "sewed with her toes, cut out paper patterns and performed other ingenious feats with her toes," A Mr. Scott Surtees, writing in *Notes and Queries* for September 22, 1888, clinched the matter by declaring that he had actually *seen* Miss Biffin's toes!

That she did possess legs is an undoubted fact, but the extent to which she was capable of using her toes is far from certain. As far as her painting was concerned, her method was invariable. She always used a long-handled brush which she took from the table with her tongue and, placing the end under a loop or pin on her right shoulder, manipulated it with her mouth. A newspaper account of the day comments: "So exquisite is that lady's touch that she can with ease tie a knot on a single hair with her tongue."

With the death of the Earl of Morton things began to go badly with Sarah. Gradually her patrons fell away and there was no longer anyone with influence to help her obtain orders for her pictures. Round about 1842 she came to Liverpool and after living in lodgings in various parts of the town settled down at Number 8 Duke Street. Here, at the age of 63, she found herself in very poor circumstances with nothing but the Civil List pension of £12 a year granted to her by William IV. To make matters worse, her eyesight began to fail and she suffered from general bodily infirmity. Fortunately, her plight came to the notice of Richard Rathbone and it was through his kindly exertions on her behalf that a sum was subscribed in order to purchase a small annuity for her.

She died at Duke Street on October 2, 1850, aged 66.

A tablet which was set up beside her grave said of her:

"Few have passed through the vale of life so much the child of hapless fortune as the deceased: and yet possessor of mental endowments of no ordinary kind. Gifted with singular talents as an artist, thousands have been gratified with the able productions of her pencil! Whilst versatile conversation and agreeable manner elicited the admiration of all. This tribute to one so universally admired is paid by those who were best acquainted with the character it so briefly portrays..." And surely those of us who knew her not at all but are acquainted with her inspiring achievements will echo with sincerity the pronouncements of her epitaph.

8. THE STORY OF SKITTLES—

FROM MERSEYSIDE TO MAYFAIR

If you had been in the habit of walking in London's Hyde Park during the early nineteen-hundreds, you would almost certainly have encountered a partially blind and very deaf old lady in a bath-chair. It is doubtful, however, if you would have realised that the tired, frail, old body in the wheel-chair was that same body which, nearly half a century before, perched gracefully upon horseback and cantering at a spanking pace along Rotten Row, and set our great-grandfather's hearts aflutter in their breasts and made its owner the toast of London town. You would, in fact, have been looking at Skittles, the last of the great courtesans.

Born Catherine Walters, in 1839, Skittles was the daughter of Liverpool-Irish parents, and first saw the light of day in the slums of Liverpool. Her father was a customs officer who, hearing the call of the sea, went into the merchant navy. He did well in the service and rumour has it that he had attained to the rank of captain before his retirement to Cheshire, where he became the landlord of an inn. Encouraged by the sporting gentry who came to the inn for refreshment after the meets of the local hounds, the young Catherine soon learned to ride and life for her was pleasant indeed until the sudden death of her father. A feckless Irishman, Captain Walters left behind not only two little girls, but also a mountain of debts in order to honour which all his effects had to be sold. And the children were sent back to Liverpool to the home of their grandmother.

Shortly after her sixteenth birthday, Catherine took a job in a Liverpool pothouse known as the Black Jack Tavern, where, apart from pulling the beer-engines and setting-up pints, her duties also included the setting-up of nine-pins in the skittle-alley, and it was here that she first received the nickname "Skittles" which was to stick to her all her life.

By the time she was seventeen, Skittles had decided that there was no future in a life that was all beer and skittles, and she betook herself to London. There she rapidly became what we call today, with ironic inexactitude, a "good-time girl" and began to amass a respectable (financially speaking!) bank balance.

Among the high spots of the London of that time was Kate Hamilton's—a glittering saloon situated in the basement of a building near Leicester Square—which was the Mecca of the roistering "swells" and their crinolined ladies. Such a place was bound to appeal to Skittles, and it was there, a couple of years after her arrival in London, that she was offered a position in the employ of a well-known livery-stableman. It was her job to act as a kind of advertisement by pubicly putting his horses through their paces. With her lovely face and trim figure, Skittles filled the bill to perfection, and it was not long before she was generally recognised as one of the prettiest of the "pretty horse-breakers"—and heart-breakers—in Hyde Park.

Moreover, her rise in the social scale was meteoric. Men flocked about her and soon she was to be seen in every fashionable haunt. On the arms of wealthy suitors, she graced the best restaurants; her photograph, like that of a modern film star, gazed from the windows of high-class photographers all over town; she even began to sway feminine fashion and the pork-pie hat which she designed for riding wear became all the go. Naturally, there were many ladies who pretended to view Skittles with the utmost contempt. But it was contempt tinged with envy, and despite the jealousy of her female detractors, and whatever may have been their opinions as to her morals, there was no gainsaying that she was a really first-rate horsewoman. On one occasion she amazed everyone, and incidentally won a £100 bet, by jumping her horse over the railings in Hyde Park. Again, at the Grand National Hunt Steeplechase at Market Harborough, she cleared, out of sheer high spirits, an 18-foot water-jump which had already claimed three victims among the competitors!

Adroit on horseback, Skittles was also an outstandingly skilful whip and her progress through Hyde Park was always watched by admiring crowds. "About 6 p.m.", writes a contemporary, "a rumour arises that Anonyma is coming. Expectation is raised to its highest pitch; a handsome woman drives rapidly by in a carriage drawn by thoroughbred ponies of surpassing shape and action; the driver is attired in the pork-pie hat and the Poole paletot introduced by Anonyma. But, alas! she causes no effect at all, for she is not Anonyma. She is only the Duchess of A———, the Marchioness of B———, the Countess of C———, or some other of Anonyma's many eager imitators. The crowd, disappointed, reseat themselves and wait . . . At last, their patience is rewarded. Anonyma and her ponies appear, and they are satisfied. She threads her way dexterously, with an unconscious air, through the throng, commented upon by hundreds who admire her and hundreds who envy her. She pulls up her ponies to speak to an acquaintance, and her carriage is instantly surrounded by a multitude; she turns and drives back again towards Apsley House; and then away into the unknown world, nobody knows whither."

It was on Rotten Row that Skittles managed to scrape up an acquaintance with Spencer Compton, Marquis of Hartington and heir to the Duke of Devonshire. Curiously enough, he had been amongst those who, years before, had come to the parlour of her father's inn. He would not remember her, but she certainly remembered him and the tales she had heard of his immense wealth. Maybe it was no accident, therefore, when her horse collided with his and threw her on the ground literally at his feet. He, in turn, fell for her, and within a very short space of time the erstwhile pothouse drudge was comfortably established in a house of her own in Park Street, Mayfair, where, with horses, carriage and servants she played hostess at Sunday afternoon baccarat parties which became the fashionable rendezvous of the aristocracy including the young Prince of Wales.

The Royal Academy Exhibition of 1861 included a picture by Landseer—*The Taming of the Shrew*. Although Sir Edwin, late President of the Royal Academy, put it about that an eminently respectable equitation instructess had been the model, it was universally recognised as the speaking likeness of the unspeakable Skittles.

In 1862 the World Exhibition was held at South Kensington and Skittles, thinking no doubt that it might also bring *her* considerable trade from overseas, decided that she must have her Mayfair house redecorated that it might be the more worthy of the many wealthy foreign visitors whom she hoped to entertain. The dining-room was made a dream of crimson repp and fat gilt cupids; the decor for the drawing-room was vivid cerise silk; her bedroom, that intimate holy of holies, was all heavenly saxe-blue silk. Even the "smallest room" boasted swansdown upholstery!

On July 3rd, 1862, a letter appeared in *The Times* lamenting that: "Thousands returning from the Exhibition, are intolerably delayed by the crowd collected to gaze on this pretty creature and her pretty ponies." It went on to ask plaintively: "Could not you, Sir, whose business it is to know everything and everybody, and who possibly therefore may know Anonyma herself, prevail on her to drive in some other portion of the Park as long as the Exhibition lasts?" This letter provoked a positive deluge of correspondence initiated by "A Belgravian Mother" who waxed indignant regarding the "involuntary virginity imposed on her own unmarried daughters by the presence of these usurpers, with attractive exteriors and accommodating morals." On the other hand, Lord Llanover, the First Commissioner, was being, at the same time, earnestly requested to provide a greater number of seats for the public in order to take the weight off the feet of those of Skittle's admirers who found the long wait for her appearances rather fatiguing! As a matter of fact those who wrote desiring Skittle's withdrawal had their wish, for soon after this she disappeared and the Ladies' Mile in Hyde Park was no longer congested.

Rumour had it that Skittles had eloped with Hartington who had gone to America. Actually, she was taking the waters at Ems and when she learned of her protector's decession she impulsively followed him to the

New World. When she confronted him at his New York hotel she got a very frigid reception and, defeated, she fled, her visions of becoming Duchess of Devonshire fading with the New York skyline. The Park Street house was sold and Skittles, after living for a time in Paris, spent several years wandering about Europe until, tired at last of this nomadic life, she returned to London in 1872.

Back in her old haunts, Skittles was delighted to find that she was still a famous figure, for during her absence three yellowback biographies had invested her name with an enchantment for thousands who had never known her in the old days. Moreover, now ten years older, she discovered that her tempestuous petticoat had been canonized by an unexpected latterday acceptance. She rented houses in South Street, Mayfair, in still-fashionable Tunbridge Wells and in Paris and took apartments in Brown's Hotel for herself and her sister Mary-Ann. Her famous parties were resumed and—surely respectability could go no further than this—Mr. Gladstone himself came, after sending her 12 lbs. of Russian tea, to take a dish of tea with her.

Skittles never married, though latterly she was known by the courtesy-title of Mrs. Baillie, but in middle-age the volatile enchantress came as near to falling in love as her essentially unromantic temperament would allow. The object of her affection was the Honourable Gerald Saumarez. She first met him while he was still at Eton and she was more than twice his age, but a bond of deep affection united them right up to the time of her death forty-one years later.

It was on a sweltering August afternoon in 1920 that the end came. Skittles had a stroke while out in her wheel-chair and was carried unconscious into the South Street house in which during those last years she had been living alone save for one old servant. It was now a ghostly place of locked rooms, drawn blinds, dust sheets and old memories, where Skittles spent most of her time in her bedroom except for that daily outing, weather permitting, to Hyde Park, the scene of her past triumphs. Her only visitors were Saumarez, her doctor and a Roman Catholic priest, for abandoning the apolaustic philosophy of her youth, Skittles had latterly embraced again the sterner faith of her childhood. And when, two days later, she died, at the ripe old age of eighty-one, it was the faithful Gerald who saw to it that Liverpool's wandering daughter had her last wish and was laid to rest in the beautiful little burial-ground of the Franciscan monastery at Crawley, Sussex.

9. THE PUGNACIOUS VICAR OF ST. GEORGE'S

There can be no doubt about it; the Reverend James Kelly, last incumbent but one of St. George's Church, which stood until the early years of this century upon the site now occupied by the Queen Victoria Memorial, was an eccentric.

Of countenance "gloomily cynical . . . its only frequent variation being the transition from a hard, dark frown to a bitter sardonic smile," he was a spare-built man, so small in stature that he had to stand upon a specially-constructed platform in order to see over the top of his own pulpit. Yet he was a fighting Irishman to his finger-tips, concealing the heart of a lion within the body of a mouse.

The Reverend Mr. Kelly came to Liverpool in 1863 and his stormy ministry continued right up to the day of his death, on March 2nd, 1892, in his eighty-sixth year. The first indication of the man's pugnacious nature was not long in manifesting itself. It was in 1864 that a Hebrew gentleman named Charles Mozley was elected mayor. Now this election did not at all accord with the Reverend Kelly's ideas, and he lost no time in letting it be known far and wide that he regarded it as most iniquitous that a non-Christian, no matter how fine and public-spirited a man he might be, should become the head of a Christian community.

Of course everyone is entitled to his own beliefs, but it was to say the least somewhat tactless to blazon such unpopular opinions abroad, especially if the church of which you hold the chaplaincy happens to be one which for upwards of a century has been the official corporation church of Liverpool. Mr. Kelly had, therefore, no one but himself to blame when, one fine Sunday morning shortly after his denunciation of the mayor-elect from his pulpit, the state procession marched determinedly past his church and, turning left into Lord Street, proceeded on its way to St. Peter's.

From that day forward the fate of St. George's was sealed, and the church, hitherto the place of worship of a large and fashionable congregation, fell into a gradual decline.

But far from learning his lesson, the vicar of St. George's now embarked upon a career so unorthodox and belligerent that he soon found himself one of the most unpopular men in Liverpool. Indeed, such was the dislike in which he was held that it even extended to his church, and before he had been twenty-four hours in his grave in Smithdown Road Cemetery, a meeting of the Finance Committee was already asking if something could not be done to abolish "the edifice which had long since ceased to be of any account in the church life of Liverpool."

A gauge of public opinion is afforded by the fact that even in those days of fulsome obituaries the newspapers commented upon his demise in the following unequivocal terms: "The Reverend James Kelly has quitted a scene in which he was never applauded."

And yet there were those who apparently thought very highly of this extraordinary cleric. The cabmen, for instance, who had a stand in the immediate vicinity of St. George's, would never hear a word against him. One of them told of receiving from his hands an unsolicited gift of 4 cwt. of coal when times were hard. Many others pointed out that he was always most concerned for their comfort, going so far as to erect a small structure at one end of his church wherein light refreshments and copies of sundry religious tracts were dispensed free of charge to cabbies and any others whom he thought stood in need. Unfortunately, this cabman's shelter had to be removed because, having built without corporation permission, it constituted a breach of official building regulations. Needless to say, its subsequent removal sent the affronted Mr. Kelly into paroxysms of anger and convinced him that a wanton Corporation was once again getting at him. The records do not state whether he actually lawed the city fathers or not on this occasion, but if he did it would have been no new thing, for, apart from his love of a fight, the Reverend James Kelly liked nothing so much as a good burst of litigation. So frequently did he have recourse to the courts that his very living became imperilled and there were wags who said that he only did it because he wished to keep up a personal acquaintance with the judges! The latter, by the way, came to regard him as a terrible nuisance for, conducting his own cases, he was forever arousing their wrath by the most flagrant breaches of all justiciary discipline.

As the years slipped by, this singular incumbent of St. George's became more and more embittered. He seemed to have the notion that every man's hand was raised against him and no one could talk to him for five minutes without discovering his peculiar characteristics. He, who was by birth and extraction an Irishman, fiercely repudiated his nationality, and loudly insisted that he was a hundred per cent. Englishman. He thought the knell of England's greatness had been sounded when a Government proposed that an iconoclast should be allowed to affirm on entering the House of Commons, and had very definite views as to the Corporation's plain duty in the matter of paying his organist!

Latterly, he took to living, with scant domestic comforts, in the vestry of his church, and preached wild, rambling and vaguely libellous sermons. Starting with some perfectly legitimate point of Scripture, he would almost immediately forget or abandon it and launch forth into a lengthy condemnation of some matter of topical interest, or descant interminably upon the virtue of any privately held opinion which came first to mind. Occasionally, he would vary the proceedings by reading long extracts from books and documents in the middle of a sermon. He had an especial liking for Acts of Parliament and would intone clause after clause with great unction and evident personal enjoyment. Such discursions served no apparently useful purpose other than to lengthen the weary space of his discourse. And yet, for all the weirdness of his ideas, and despite the huge posters of startlingly-worded warnings with which he plastered the walls of his church, this old-fashioned evangelical parson was by no means the unmitigated crank which many people thought him.

An ardent follower of Calvin, he was also a sound Hebrew scholar and a considerable expert upon prophecy and inspiration. Himself an outcast, he had always a sympathetic ear for the pleas of the fallen and the distressed, and as one who knew him well wrote after his death: "When you knew him there was something curiously majestic in the solemn, calm, firm manner in which this reverend old gentleman marched to his ends, or towards them, pronouncing all the time with affectionate severity the doom of all who stood in his way."

An eccentric he may have been, but he was a type who would face up to any opposition, no matter how fierce or fearful. He was made of the stuff of the martyrs and would undoubtedly have gone to the stake in defence of his highly individual principles without repining. It is perhaps unfortunate that an accident of circumstances made him a man at war with the world at a time when persecution lit no fires.

10. THE STRANGE CLAIMS OF MARGARET M'AVOY

From time to time in the history of most towns there emerges from obscurity some enigmatic figure whose curious claims to this or that supernatural power make of him a nine-day's wonder. For a little while the strange one becomes the notorious cynosure of all eyes, and then, just as suddenly, falls back into the rut of normality out of which he has so ephemerally climbed.

Such a one was Margaret M'Avoy, a 17-year-old girl, who, in the high summer of 1817, had all Liverpool in a state of frantic excitement.

Up to the age of sixteen, Margaret M'Avoy, who lived in St Paul's Square, was just a normal, healthy girl, but during the year 1816 she was suddenly stricken with attacks of partial paralysis and water on the brain and as a result of these afflictions was said by her medical attendants to have gone completely blind.

That was on or about June 7th, 1816.

On June 28th, Margaret's mother first set the sightless girl to do some needlework. She began by knitting a stocking and it seems that in the course of the following July she mastered the awkward technique of working blind so successfully that by the end of that month she was not only darning silk gloves with the most extraordinary neatness, but was actually able to make her own frocks.

One day in early September a chance conversation took place between a Mr. and Mrs. Hughes respecting St. Thomas à Becket, and Margaret M'Avoy who happened to be present said that before going blind she had seen an account of his life in a book called *The Lives of the Saints* and added that if she had the book she could point out the place where it occurred. In the circumstances it was a rather strange statement, but the volume was quickly found and placed in her hands. The girl turned its pages over slowly until she came to the passage in question and then calmly proceeded to "read" a few words of the text. Naturally, the Hughes's were very surprised by this performance, and Mr. Hughes jocularly asked Margaret if she could *feel* the letters with her fingers. To this, the girl replied that she had indeed felt the words and said that if her father would give her another book she would try to read something else. A large folio Bible was promptly produced and, running her finger carefully along the lines, Margaret began, to the utter astonishment of everyone, to "read" several of the verses.

The very next day Miss M'Avoy demonstrated her fantastic faculty before a number of strangers who visited her parents' house and to allay any suspicion of trickery she wore a thick bandage over her eyes. The news of these strange events spread like wildfire and it was not long before the quiet house in St. Paul's Square was packed every day with throngs of wondering people.

The weeks passed and gradually Margaret M'Avoy discovered that this amazing power of perception was not confined to her fingers alone, but that she could also distinguish the colours of objects which were brought into contact with the backs of her hands. But side by side with this latest phenomenon there developed a peculiar periodic suspension of her powers which always manifested itself in company with a sensation of extreme coldness in her fingers. Miss M'Avoy also said that she had found that any obstruction between her mouth and nostrils produced a similar suspension and explained this by saying that her breath had to have free and uninterrupted communication with her hands.

In the October, Margaret M'Avoy was taken to be examined at the house of a Mr. John Latham, a surgeon, at Wavertree, where, despite—or maybe because of—the presence of no less than five physicians and several surgeons, no satisfactory decision could be reached as to whether she was in fact blind or not. One at least of these medical gentlemen was thoroughly convinced of her absolute genuineness. This was the eminent Dr. Renwick who actually went so far as to publish a pamphlet affirming his complete faith in what he described as her "new and supernatural faculty."

Thus encouraged, Miss M'Avoy progressed to ever more startling attainments. Not only did she read with her hands behind her back and under the bedclothes, but now she was telling the time by simply feeling the glass of a watch.

About March 18th, 1817, her overworked fingers became "short-sighted" and thereafter a magnifying glass had to be applied to those members if she was required to read any small print!

It was round about this time, too, that she discovered "agitation" as one of the prime causes of the coldness and subsequent suspension. This was in many respects a most fortunate discovery, for, being a sensitive girl, she was easily agitated, and if anyone doubted her veracity and disputed her powers it always agitated her. Tests of any kind also agitated her and, very conveniently, made her correspondingly less able to give those very proofs to secure which the test was designed.

Nevertheless, it was proved by several of those tests which she so heartily disliked that she was unable to exercise her uncanny gifts in the dark.

It was on August 4th 1817, that her powers reached their apogee. Upon that afternoon, in the presence of a large number of spectators, she turned her back to the window and, placing her hands upon its glass, she described in detail the appearance and activities of a number of workmen in the churchyard across the road. Unfortunately, the scientific value of this performance is somewhat negated by the fact that the whole scene was clearly reflected in a particularly handsome mirror which hung upon the wall opposite the window!

Shortly after this, Miss M'Avoy received a visit from a Mr. Egerton Smith. This gentleman's advent was to prove her undoing, for he brought with him a most ingeniously-contrived mask, so constructed that whilst entirely covering the eyes and face it left her mouth and nostrils quite free.

"It is my opinion," said Mr. Smith, "that wearing this mask Miss M'Avoy will be unable to read a single line of even moderately-sized print, but if she can I will gladly pay her twenty guineas."

"And I'll double it," chimed in another equally sceptical bystander.

It may be that on hearing mention of all that money the "agitation" became too much for the poor girl! Anyway, despite these handsome offers, she steadfastly declined to undergo the proposed test and that was the end of Miss M'Avoy.

Today, the wonder of it all is that a 17-year-old girl should have been so incredibly successful in fooling so many people for so long a time. Doubtless, it was the fact that no money was ever asked for—although Miss M'Avoy did receive a number of presents and openly admitted that she "*felt* gold and silver to be more pleasant than brass"—together with the respectable position of her parents, that contributed largely to those who found themselves genuinely puzzled according to her the benefit of their doubt. Seen in perspective, the problem resolves itself as a psychological rather than a physiological one and it is virtually certain that the whole affair stemmed out of a young girl's hysterical desire for notoriety.

11. HUGH OWEN THOMAS—SURGEON EXTRAORDINARY

Within a hundred yards of where I once lived and worked there is a grave wherein lies all that was mortal of one of the most extraordinary and gifted men who ever served the noble cause of medicine in the city of Liverpool. This man was Hugh Owen Thomas, and his was no mere local celebrity; he occupies a position of considerable eminence in the pages of the history of medicine, as the founder of British *orthopaedics, and is likewise assured of a permanent place in the bizarre ranks of the English eccentrics. He was in every sense a surgeon extraordinary.

During the middle and latter years of the last century, Hugh Owen Thomas was a familiar figure in Liverpool, driving in his scarlet dog-cart through the myriad dockside streets, lending a splash of colourful relief to their squalid monotony. Day in day out, year in year out, the slight, nervously energetic doctor with the goatee beard would rise at 6 o'clock and, after a frugal breakfast of tea and bananas, set forth on his interminable rounds. His clothes were as invariable as his habits. Always the long, heavy ulster, buttoned up to the collar, the stout gauntleted gloves, and, because of a weak left eye, the peaked nautical cap, pulled well down over that injured member. From his lip drooped an eternal cigarette, and this in the days long before it was the common form of tobacco addiction! Rumour had it that the cigarette habit was first acquired by him as a measure to ward off the likelihood of infection during a cholera epidemic, and that, the demon Nicotine taking possession of his soul, he had never since relinquished it. He was a lonely man, this quaint, Welsh doctor, and had little to do with his fellow-medicos, as much from lack of an instinct for sociability as from the lack of time which his strenuous time-table implied. In short, he was an exile by choice, and preferred a life of unremitting labour among the denizens of Dockland, to the society of the self-styled "superior classes" whose ideas and ideals he held in contempt. He was an original and heartily despised the conventions and the conventional.

This strange man was the son of a Welsh farmer, Evan Thomas, who in the year 1830 had come to Liverpool from the Isle of Anglesey, where for generations the Thomases had wrested a hard-won living from a stony soil. They were always a rather curious family, amply endowed with the fiery eloquence of their race; preachers and minor poets of no mean calibre. But aside from all this, they were far-famed among the men of the hillside community as rural healers—men in whose strong hands there resided a strange power of healing all manner of aches, sprains and fractures. Evan

*Orthopaedics is that branch of medicine which is concerned with the correction of deformities, and the treatment of chronic diseases of the joints and the spine.

Thomas, grown tired of the life of the farm and an initiate in the hereditary secrets of the family curative cult, finding himself an adept in the practice of the bone-setter, decided then to transform the family hobby into a personal profession. He selected as the site of his venture the then new dockland of Liverpool. This was a wise if somewhat obvious choice, for here, where the newly-weaned first-born of the industrial revolution swarmed in their inconsequent thousands, would be practice in abundance. If tragedies there were amidst the green, smiling hills of Anglesey, how much more likely that accidents and hideous injuries should abound where the face of nature was smoked and dark, burst and ruptured by the machinery of money-making; where men and women and an amplitude of hapless children lived in gloom and dankness, often inadequately fed, and bedded in the very lap of disease. Here was labour indeed for the wonder-working hands! And so it proved, for Evan Thomas built up a very considerable practice among the rough diamonds of the seaport, and if his work in his Crosshall Street surgery earned him the love and respect of grateful patients, his successes excited the jealousy and barely half-hid scorn of the diploma'd fraternity of surgeons who cried "Charlatan" loud and long. His enemies were ever watchful, and three times he was prosecuted for manslaughter; three times he left the court triumphant. But Evan Thomas was too shrewd a man to imagine that his own successes were a guarantee of perpetual inviolability, and resolved that the next generation of Thomases should perpetuate the family tradition from the protective shelter of the cloak of an orthodox medical degree. He had five sons all of whom he sent to study medicine at Edinburgh University. The eldest of these was Hugh Owen Thomas, frail and talented, at the same time scientist and fanatic. Here in the shadow of the great Lister, he spent hard years of conscientious industry, studying his text-books, walking the wards, apprenticed to the art of fighting nature in a malignant mood.

In 1858, after brief sojourns in the wards of Paris and London, Hugh Owen Thomas returned to Liverpool a fully fledged doctor. At first he lived with his father, but the following year the latter remarried, and, apparently disapproving of his stepmother, Thomas departed for ever from the parental abode.

The young Dr. Thomas set forth in search of a suitable residence. It was characteristic of the man that disdaining Rodney Street (the Harley Street of Liverpool) he settled upon a large house in Nelson Street. Today, Nelson Street is little else than a dilapidated back street, and it is strange to reflect as you walk its decadent length, that it was here in this grimly grimy thoroughfare that British orthopaedics were born and efficiently cradled.

The house had to be large as it was at once residence, surgery and workshop, for Thomas employed a blacksmith and a saddler in the manufacture of the various irons, splints and other mechanical devices which were the products of his inventive genius. It was also necessary that his consulting room should be one of exceptional size in order to accommodate the ailing crowds who flocked to him. The arrangement of the surgery was upon a somewhat novel plan. There was a number of cubicles so that one patient might be undressing whilst the doctor was actually examining another: Thomas's time was precious. In the centre of the surgery stood a most fearsome-looking machine for the reducing of fractures of the shoulder. The patient sat in a steel chair while the master-craftsman clicked the injured bone back into position. Thomas was showman enough to realise the psychological value of impressing his patients with his amazing dexterity, and would allow those who were awaiting his ministrations to watch him at work. Once set in its splint, Thomas guarded against the possibility of anyone tampering with his handiwork by the simple expedient of sealing all the fastenings with wax embossed with his own signet-ring.

Generally speaking, his patients were rather scared of the sharp, mercurial doctor, whose eyes gleamed piercingly at them from beneath the peak of his fantastic cap. He was brusque in manner, and gave orders that were concise and determined and brooked no argument. Many are the stories which are told of his curious methods. One lady who suffered from a defect of the spine was brought to him by her anxious husband. Thomas curtly ordered her to undress and left the room. A few minutes later he returned and, rushing at her without a word of warning, delivered her a terrific kick on the backside. He then told her husband to take her home. The kick had had the desired effect; the spine had snapped back into its rightful position. On another occasion the brother of a friend of mine was taken to Dr. Thomas because a broken arm had knitted together incorrectly. The doctor examined the frightened child and told him to remove his shirt. He then left the cubicle and, returning a minute or two later by another door behind the boy's back, he rushed at him and, taking the fragile arm in his powerful hands, snapped the brittle bone in two. Before the child had time to realise what had happened, Thomas had disappeared again like a whirlwind. It must be remembered that all this was in the days before the common use of anaesthetics, and Thomas evidently believed in the effectiveness of surprise rather than the palliation of anaesthesia.

Despite these alarming and altogether unorthodox procedures, Dr. Thomas was never short of patients. Indeed they came to him far more readily than they would trust themselves to a hospital. He was appointed medical officer to no less than twenty-eight Workers' Friendly Societies and it must be admitted that, for all his queerness, he achieved a very high percentage of successes. Thomas was by no means a wealthy man. He was not interested in money and gave away pretty well everything that he had saved. It was, however, a matter of principle with him to insist that every patient, no matter how poor, should pay him some sort of fee. This is another example of his sound knowledge of practical psychology for he realised that people will always tend to underestimate the value of the easily acquired. A grim little tale is told of how once, when he had put a dislocated shoulder back in place, a disgruntled patient complained at the exorbitant charge of five shillings for what seemed to him to have been a very simple operation. "Too much is it?" snapped Dr. Thomas. "Well, we'll soon put the shoulder out again for you." We may be sure that the complaining one paid up without further ado!

Of course Hugh Owen Thomas was a general practitioner and had to deal with a number of cases other than those orthopaedic ones which were his especial delight. He was particularly skilled in the treatment of intestinal obstructions and developed a system of internal orthopaedics. A visit from him was an awe-inspiring experience. You could never be sure at what time of the day or night the little Welshman would materialize at your bedside in a cloud of cigarette smoke. He would sweep down the street in his brilliant phaeton, silently unlatch the front door, and make his way to the sickroom in a matter of minutes. The lynx eyes noted everything, though it was his custom to ignore everyone in the house other than the sufferer, and woe-betide the relative or attendant who had neglected to carry out his orders to the last drop of water; the caustic tongue would lash them unmercifully. Among the simple and uneducated Merseysiders, his downright frightfulness was an asset earning him the respect of some, the fear of others, and the whole-hearted confidence of all. Reared as a strict Calvinist, Thomas broke away from the faith of his fore-fathers and became an agnostic. Yet none could call him an irreligious man, and it seemed almost that he treated his very agnosticism as a religion. Every Sunday morning he held a free clinic at his Nelson Street house, and he appeared to derive a sardonic pleasure from working to the accompaniment of the iron-tongued church-bells. This sacrifice of hard-earned leisure to charity was in reality Christianity at its best. Christianity in a practical form, shorn of much cant, and one feels sure that the Master Healer could not in His Wisdom and Justice condemn this charitable infidel. In those days there were no clinics or out-patient departments at hospitals and the only government health department, the General Board of Health, had crumbled before the onslaught of the reactionaries in Parliament. National Health was the concern of no one in particular. In such circumstances it may well be imagined what a blessing Thomas's free clinic proved to the legions of the overworked and underpaid who could not afford to be away from work an hour longer than was absolutely essential

As the laborious years slipped over his rapidly greying head, Thomas's fame spread far and wide. Popular fancy wove a strange web of legend around the austere figure and popular credence attributed to him the mastery of white magic. Among his medical colleagues, however, his genius passed unrecognised. The University Medical Faculty ignored his existence, and he was never appointed to the staff of any hospital. This general neglect was in a large measure his own fault. He would not go out of his way to curry favour with the influential and indeed, spared himself no pains to make lifelong enemies of those who disagreed with him. Moreover, he consistently refused all invitations to address medical conferences, though in private he never lost an opportunity of preaching his gospel of the curative efficacy of rest. He was always careful, however, to insist that the rest-period should not be so prolonged as to result in a permanent stiffness. Apart from the odd article in the *Lancet*, the few medical articles and books which he produced were printed by a jobbing printer round the corner and published at his own expense. It never occurred to him to worry if anyone read them, but nevertheless his *magnum opus*, somewhat cumbrously entitled, *Knee, Hip and Ankle*, reached America where it was hailed as a revolutionary work. It brought many an admirer from the other side of the Atlantic on a hurried pilgrimage to the lonely pioneer of Nelson Steet. And as spring turned to summer, and autumn to winter in the eternal yet never monotonous panorama of the seasons, Thomas worked on at fever-pitch. He scorned delights and lived laborious days. It was almost as though he was deliberately and desperately trying to cheat time, lashed into a frenzy by some Celtic premonition that his days were numbered. There was so much to do and time so short. From 6 o'clock in the morning until late at night, when his wife would play his favourite soporific, the "Dead March in Saul," to him, he scarcely stopped.

Thomas must have realised that even his iron constitution could not withstand indefinitely such gross misuse and he began to cast about for some one to train to carry on the practice. His choice fell upon his nephew, Robert Jones, then attending the Liverpool Medical School. So began a fateful partnership. A partnership which rescued Thomas's methods from that oblivion to which their eccentric inventor's taciturn secretiveness would inevitably have condemned them. When Thomas died in 1891 at the age of 57, a man worn out by incessant labours, it was this boy, later Sir Robert Jones, who was to bring his uncle's pioneer work to its glorious culmination and make the drab old house in Nelson Street the Mecca of British orthopaedics. He it was, too, who introduced "Thomas's Splint" which not only saved many limbs but was also directly responsible for the reducing of the death rate from compound fractures of the thigh-bone from 80 per cent. to 20 per cent.

When, in 1933, Sir Robert Jones died, his body was laid to rest in Liverpool Cathedral; his passing was the end of an epoch—the epoch of the "scientific bone-setter." Today, Liverpool University has its professor of orthopaedics and the subject has become an important and ever-progressive branch of modern medicine. There is new hope for the child-victims of tuberculosis and rickets, the descendants of the poor, deformed children who fed the dim old surgery in Nelson Street. The tiny spark which was ignited in the consulting cubicles of Hugh Owen Thomas has become a vast purifying fire.

But for the arch-craftsman who passed unmourned by the men of orthodox medicine there is no magnificent cathedral tomb. Deep in the quiet earth lies Hugh Owen Thomas in the grave in Liverpool's Toxteth cemetery, whither, more than ninety years ago, a thousand mourners followed his funeral cortège. He was always a poor man's doctor and it was the poor, the ignorant, who, with surer instincts than the great, the enlightened men of medicine, bemourned the passing of a master-surgeon. A strange band of dockland roughs and toughs, with many a red-rimmed eye to belie the apparent harshness of their faces. His monument is not the tall polished-granite tombstone—symbol of death—but rather the work he left behind, the legacy which every day bestows new life and hope to the lame and the halt. The blind—his contemporary professional brethren—have in the fulness of time had their eyes opened too.

12. SIR ROBERT JONES—BELOVED PHYSICIAN

In the year 1873 a fifteen-year-old boy alighted from a four-wheeler at the door of Number 11 Nelson Street, Liverpool. The lad had come from London to the house of his uncle, the famous and eccentric surgeon-cum-bone-setter, Hugh Owen Thomas, to be initiated into the manners and mysteries of the profession of medicine. There may seem to have been nothing unusual in the arrival of this youth, unheralded, unobserved, and yet, for all the apparent insignificance of the occasion, it was, in fact, destined to be an event of world-wide importance; not only was it to secure an undying fame for Hugh Owen Thomas but, and this was more important, it was to ensure the preservation and wide adoption of those curative methods which were to prove the veritable foundations of British orthopaedics.

The name of the young disciple of Destiny was Robert Jones, and he it was whom Fate had chosen to write the second chapter in the Nelson Street Saga. Indeed, but for his uncle's interest in the boy, the pioneer work of Hugh Owen Thomas might well have perished with his untimely death and the great volume of his labours never have expanded into the glorious triumph of revolutionised orthopaedics which the united genius of Thomas and Jones finally achieved.

Robert Jones was accordingly enrolled at Liverpool Medical School and spent the next six years in absorbing his theoretical training at that establishment and in receiving rigorous practical instruction in his uncle's surgery. He duly qualified in 1878. The twenty-one-year-old doctor then became assistant to Thomas, in which capacity he gained invaluable opportunities for the observation of the unusual injuries which were a prominent feature of his uncle's dockland practice.

In 1881 Jones was appointed Honorary Assistant Surgeon at the Stanley Hospital and in 1885 he decided to set up in practice for himself at 22 Great George Square. His previous experience of injuries to manual workers stood him in good stead and throughout the building of the Manchester Ship Canal (1887-1893) he acted as consulting surgeon. To assess the cost in human life of such an engineering feat must have been very interesting and it is recorded that more than 3,000 accidents occurred.

Thomas died in 1891 and Jones took over the old surgery in Nelson Street and entered into a phase of incredible activity. It really seemed as though some part of the spirit of the old man had taken up its abode within the body of his genial, easy-going nephew. For years his daily routine consisted of breakfast at 7-30 a.m. and twenty-six operations between lunch and 9 p.m. Not to mention some 7,000 patients a year whom he saw at his free clinic, held at his house every Sunday in the tradition of his uncle. Despite the huge demands of all this professional labour, he somehow managed to find time for shooting, riding, boxing, cricket and the indulgence of his passion for entertaining.

He introduced many innovations at Nelson Street including Tom, the butler, who became almost as famous among the patients as his master. Nor was he neglectful of medical advances and the first X-Ray photograph ever taken in this country was made at Nelson Street in 1895.

Jones's fame spread far and wide. By this time he had begun to specialise in orthopaedic cases and patients came from all over the country to consult him. Among the many well-known people who sought his advice was Buffalo Bill Cody. That grand old showman found a kindred spirit in Robert Jones and, with an appropriate show of dignity, presented him with a pistol. Occasionally some hero from the boxing ring would come for his ministrations. Once, an eminent pugilist, who shall be nameless, called and was told by Jones to lie down on the floor. He did so, whereupon Jones gave vent to a great guffaw at the same time remarking, "Oh! Mr. ————, how often have I seen you in this position?"

A large number of Jones's patients were children and it was in the handling of these poor little cripples that he excelled himself. Perhaps an explanation may be found in the fact that he loved all children. He had very definite ideas as to the agencies which would contribute most to their cure. They need sunshine, fresh air and play, he told himself over and over again. He remembered the bad old days when the deformed child lay lonely and pitied in a wooden packing-case with one of Thomas's torturous irons upon its wasted limb and the prospect of a life on crutches before it. He was seized with the idea of reform and, like the man of action he was, set to work to translate his dreams into reality. He became acquainted with a young woman named Agnes Hunt who kept a convalescent home for children at Baschurch. She, too, had become obsessed with the idea of open-air treatment for the little sufferers and between them they created the first orthopaedic hospital in the world in a stable and a few sheds in the heart of the lovely Shrophire countryside.

With the advent of the First World War, Jones found himself in charge of military orthopaedics, an appointment which he filled with distinction. His success may well have been due to the fact that he treated the embittered soldiers just like the frightened children from whom they differed so little in reality. The exigencies of war demanded simple apparatus for front-line use. Jones bent a piece of iron into a hoop, attached a leather ring to it, as he had seen Thomas do in the old Nelson Street days, and thus was born the "Thomas Splint," which reduced deaths from shock by 60 per cent. In 1917 he received a well-deserved knighthood for his yeoman service.

Jones continued in harness to the end and on January 14th, 1933, he died at Bodynfoel, Montgomeryshire.

His ashes were laid to rest in the Chapel of Service in Liverpool Cathedral, where a small grey tablet gives testimony to a city's cherished memory of the man of whom Lord Dawson of Penn said: "For him the thread of life was strung with the beads of thought and love."

In nearby Parliament Street, on the facade of the Sir Robert Jones Memorial Workshops, his name is written in letters of gold for all to see, but, more than that, it is written in love and gratitude in the hidden depths of the hearts of those he loved to serve.